Rashomon

Rutgers Films in Print

Mirella Jona Affron, Robert Lyons,
and E. Rubinstein, editors

My Darling Clementine, John Ford, director
edited by Robert Lyons

The Last Metro, François Truffaut, director
edited by Mirella Jona Affron and E. Rubinstein

Touch of Evil, Orson Welles, director
edited by Terry Comito

The Marriage of Maria Braun, Rainer Werner Fassbinder, director
edited by Joyce Rheuban

Letter from an Unknown Woman, Max Ophuls, director
edited by Virginia Wright Wexman, with Karen Hollinger

Rashomon, Akira Kurosawa, director
edited by Donald Richie

Rashomon

Akira Kurosawa,
director

Donald Richie, editor

Rutgers University Press

New Brunswick and London

Library of Congress Cataloging-in-Publication
Data
Rashomon
 (Rutgers films in print; v. 6)
 Translation of dialogue from the film
Rashomon.
 I. Kurosawa, Akira, 1910–
II. Richie, Donald, 1924–
III. Rashomon (Motion picture) IV. Series.
PN1997.R24313   1986   791.43'72   86–
1927
ISBN 0–8135–1179–8
ISBN 0–8135–1180–1 (pbk.)

British Cataloguing-in-Publication Information
Available

Screenplay courtesy Akira Kurosawa and Daiei
Motion Picture Co., 1950, all rights reserved.
Based on *Rashomon* by Kurosawa, Grove
Press, Inc. copyright © 1969. Stills on pages
46, 54, 56, 58, 66, and 74, courtesy Japan Film
Library. Stills on pages 16, 37, 44, 61, 73, 78,
150, and 178, courtesy The Museum of Modern
Art/Film Stills Archive. "Kurosawa: His Life
and Art" by Audie E. Bock reprinted by per-
mission of The Japan Society and Audie E.
Bock, Chief Executive Officer of East-West
Classics Films, from Japan Society catalog,
"Kurosawa: A Retrospective," 26 Films by
Akira Kurosawa presented by the Japan Film
Center of Japan Society, 1981. Excerpts from
Something Like an Autobiography by Akira
Kurosawa translated by Audie E. Bock and
from *The Waves at Genji's Door: Japan
Through Its Cinema* by Joan Mellen, reprinted
by permission of *Audie E. Bock, Joan Mellen*,
and *Alfred A. Knopf, Inc.* Reviews of
Rashomon by Bosley Crowther dated December
27, 1951 and January 6, 1952 reprinted by per-
mission of The New York Times Company,
copyright © 1951/1952. Review by Richard
Griffith in *The Saturday Review*, January 19,
1952 reprinted by permission of Gannett Foun-
dation, Inc. Review by John Beaufort reprinted
by permission of *The Christian Science Monitor*, copyright © 1952 by The Christian Science
Publishing Society. Review by John McCarten
reprinted by permission of The New Yorker
Magazine, Inc., copyright © 1951, 1979 by
The New Yorker Magazine, Inc. Review in
March 14, 1952 issue of *The Times*, reprinted
by permission of the Times Newspapers Limited, London. "*Rashomon* and the Japanese
Cinema" by Curtis Harrington, translated by
Elliott Stein, first published in *Cahiers du Cinéma* (May 1952) as "Rashomon et le Cinéma
japonais." "Rashomon and the Fifth Witness"
by George Barbarow reprinted from *The Hud-
son Review* 5, no. 3 (Autumn 1952), copyright
© 1952 by *The Hudson Review*. "Rashomon as
Modern Art" by Parker Tyler reprinted from
Three Faces of the Film, by permission, A. S.
Barnes and Company, copyright © 1960, 1967.
"Memory of Defeat in Japan" by James F.
Davidson, reprinted from *The Antioch Review*
14, no. 4 (December 1954), copyright © 1954
by The Antioch Review, Inc. "Rashomon" by
Tadao Sato, translated by Goro Sato from
Kurosawa Akira no Sekai [The World of Kuro-
sawa], Sanichi Shobo (1968), Tokyo. "The Im-
pact of Rashomon" by Stanley Kauffmann from
"Rashomon" in *Living Images*, copyright ©
1975 by Stanley Kauffmann, reprinted by permission of Brandt & Brandt Literary Agents,
Inc. "The Dialectic of Light and Darkness in
Kurosawa's *Rashomon*" by Keiko I. McDonald
reprinted from *Cinema East* (1983) by permission of Associated University Presses.

Contents

Introduction

Rashomon

Donald Richie

Kurosawa had for some time wanted to make the film that eventually became *Rashomon*. A scenario was written, a budget was determined, and then (in 1948) the picture was cancelled because the small Toyoko Company, which was to have financed it, decided it was too much of a risk. Toho—Kurosawa's company off and on for a number of years—was against it. Then Daiei signed a one-year distribution and production contract with Kurosawa.[1] He and his associates left Toho to form the short-lived Motion Picture Art Association, and one of the director's hopes was to be able to make this picture.

After completing *Scandal*, Kurosawa showed Daiei the script which became *Rashomon*. "It was a bit short . . . but all of my friends liked it very much. Daiei, however, did not understand it and kept asking: But what is it about? I made it longer, put on a beginning and an ending—and they eventually agreed to make it. Thus Daiei joined those—Shochiku for *The Idiot,* Toho for *Record of a Living Being*—who were brave enough to try something different." This is a very charitable statement. Actually Daiei was adamant in its refusal to understand. Masaichi Nagata, head of the studio and standing somewhat in relation to

This essay first appeared, in somewhat different form, in *The Films of Akira Kurosawa,* Revised Edition (Berkeley: University of California Press, 1984). The explanatory footnotes have been added by the general editors of this series.

1. For the role of such studios as Toho and Daiei in the history of Japanese film, see Joseph L. Anderson and Donald Richie, *The Japanese Film, Art and Industry,* Expanded Edition (Princeton: Princeton University Press, 1982).

Japanese film as Darryl Zanuck once stood to American production, walked out
on the first screening and, until the picture began winning prizes abroad, was
very fond of telling the press how little he understood *his* film—his, since he, in
the manner of a Goldwyn or a Zanuck, or a Wald, often signed his own name as
executive producer. Toho never gave adequate foreign distribution to *Record of a
Living Being* and Shochiku butchered *The Idiot*.

The beginnings of *Rashomon* lie in the stories of Ryunosuke Akutagawa, that
brilliant and erratic stylist who committed suicide at thirty-five in 1927. His
position in Japanese letters, though secure, has always been special—as special
as that of Poe in America or Maupassant in France. He has always been popular
and is also critically well-thought-of, almost despite his popularity. Yet he has
never been considered in the "main stream" of Japanese literature. His defenders
point out his inventive style; his detractors call him "Western" in orientation.

He *is* "Western" in the same way Kurosawa is: he is concerned with truths
which are ordinarily outside pragmatic Japanese morality and, being concerned
with them, he questions them. This he does with an involuted, elliptical style, the
essence of which is irony.

The film is based, loosely, upon two of Akutagawa's hundred-odd short stories:
the title story, "Rashomon," and "In a Grove"—which give the film its plot, or
plots. The title story has little in it that Kurosawa used, except the general description of the ruined gate, the conversation about the devastation of Kyoto
during the period of civil wars, and the atmosphere of desolation. The story, like
the film, begins in the rain. A discharged servant shelters himself under the gate,
then decides to wait in the loft for the weather to clear. There he finds an old
woman who is stealing hair from the corpses left there. She pleads that she only
steals to make a living by making wigs from the stolen hair. The servant, who has
decided to become a thief, knocks her down and takes her clothes, saying that her
defense has proved his own. He runs away and that is the end of the story.

"In a Grove" opens abruptly with the testimony of a woodcutter before the
police. This is followed by various testimonies—that of a priest, a police agent,
an old woman who turns out to be the mother of the girl the bandit raped, the
bandit himself, the girl herself, the murdered man through a medium—and there
is no conclusion: the reader is presented with seven testimonies and given no
indication of how to think about them. Akutagawa's point was the simple one that
all truth is relative, with the corollary that there is thus no truth at all.

Kurosawa's most significant addition (besides that of the abandoned baby in
the last scenes) is the introduction of the character of the commoner, a cynical yet

inquisitive man, whose questions and disbelief act as a commentary upon all the various versions of the story. The commoner talks to both priest and wood-cutter—since all three are found under the gate at the beginning of the film—and in a way acts as a moral (or amoral) chorus. He is the single person in the cast of eight (the medium herself is involved because she speaks for the dead man) who is essentially uninvolved. He alone has no story, no version to tell. It is through his questions that the film evolves.

First, the woodcutter tells how he went into the forest and found the woman's hat, some rope, an amulet-case, and then went to the police. There he recounts how he found the body. The priest's testimony follows directly. He tells how he saw the murdered man and his wife some time before. This is followed directly by the story of the police agent who tells how he managed to capture the bandit. His story is broken into by the bandit, who tells the apparent truth of his capture and continues to give the first version of the tragedy.

He was asleep under a tree when the man and his wife went past; the wind blew her veil and he saw her and decided he wanted her. He tricked the husband into following him, tied him up, went back, got the wife, raped her in front of the husband, and then turned to go, when she stopped him, saying that her honor demanded that the men now fight. In the resulting duel the bandit killed the husband and the woman ran away.

The second version is the woman's in the police court. She takes up the story after the rape, says that the bandit went away and that her own husband spurned her because she had been (presumably so easily) violated. Wild with grief she apparently kills him, then runs away and is finally found by the police.

The third version is that of the dead husband himself, speaking through the lips of a medium. He says that after the rape the bandit made overtures, wanting to take the wife away with him. She agrees and then insists that he kill the husband. This angers the bandit, who spurns her and goes away. The man finds the woman's dagger (which has been mentioned in all the earlier versions of the story) and kills himself. Much later, after he has been dead for some time, he feels someone taking the dagger away.

The fourth version is that of the woodcutter who is prevailed upon to correct his first story. He says that after the rape he found the bandit on his knees before the woman, pleading with her to go away with him. The woman says that she cannot decide, that only the men can. They are reluctant but she insists. They fight and the bandit kills the husband. She runs away and eventually the bandit also leaves. The woodcutter—whose own veracity is questioned when it transpires that *he* might have stolen the dagger, either from the ground or from the chest of the dead man—says: "I don't understand any of [them. They] don't make sense." To which the commoner replies: "Well, don't worry about [it. It] isn't as though men were reasonable."

This is more or less the point of the Akutagawa story and this is where the original stops. Kurosawa, however, goes on. Having invented the character of the commoner, having chosen to frame all of his stories within the general story of the three conversing under the ruined gate, he now invents a further incident. They hear a baby crying and the commoner finds it. He takes its clothes (a suggestion perhaps from the original "Rashomon" story), an act which horrifies the other two and which, in turn, makes him culpable. Throughout the picture he has not once acted, merely asked questions—now he acts and his act is immoral. The woodcutter picks up the naked child, saying he will take it home. The priest says that this single act has restored his faith in men and the picture concludes with the rain stopping, the sun breaking through, and the woodcutter going off with the baby.

Akutagawa is content to question all moral values, all truth. Kurosawa, obviously, is not. Neither anarchist nor misanthrope, he insists upon hope, upon the possibility of gratuitous action. Like the priest, he cannot believe that men are evil—and, indeed, if Kurosawa has a spokesman in the film it is probably the priest: weak, confused, but ultimately trusting.

There is, however, much more to the film than this. There is an apparent mystery, an elliptical intent, which has fascinated audiences all over the world. Daiei was quite right to ask what the picture was about, though its dismissal of the picture as being a kind of mystification was ill-judged. One of the most fascinating aspects of the film is just that it is extremely difficult to determine *what* it means. It shares with other modern art (abstract painting, free-form sculpture) an apparent lack of ostensible meaning which (in painting) returns to us our ability to see form and color, which (in sculpture) gives us our original vision—that of children—and lets us observe rock as rock, wood as wood, and which (in films such as *Rashomon, Muriel, Paris nous appartient*)[2] allows us to examine human action undistracted by plot, undisturbed by logic.

The central section of *Rashomon* is an anecdote presented four times, in four different ways. Each member of the triangle (bandit, woman, husband) tells a version, and the fourth is that of the only witness: the woodcutter.

2. *Muriel,* 1963, directed by Alain Resnais; *Paris nous appartient (Paris Belongs to Us),* 1960, directed by Jacques Rivette.

At first the woodcutter says only that he found the body of the husband but at the end he confesses that he saw the entire incident. Thus, it is he who might be lying. He is the only eyewitness—that is, we hear the testimony of the other three only through the priest and himself, both of whom were present at the prison questioning. We never once see the other stories directly. Everything is history— and the story is told by the two to a third, the commoner. Further, the only link between these two sets of three people is the woodcutter himself. The husband is dead, the wife and bandit are either in jail or executed for murder. In any case, all are unavailable to us. The priest only knows what he has heard the wife, bandit, and husband say. So, it comes down to the woodcutter. He is the only one who saw anything. He lied once. He may lie again.

There is a further difficulty in that we are never quite certain *who* is telling some of these apparently varying stories. A breakdown of the recountings of the anecdote gives:

1. The discovery of the body.		Told by the woodcutter.
2. Husband and wife seen in the forest.		Told by the priest.
3. The bandit's capture.	Told by the police agent.	
4. The bandit's version of the story.	Told by the bandit.	
5. The wife's version.	Told by the wife.	
6. The husband's version.	Told by the husband through the medium.	
7. The woodcutter's version.		Told by the woodcutter.

The only first-person stories are therefore those of the woodcutter and the priest, and the latter only happened to see the husband and wife (alive) in the woods. This means that he saw them before the time of the anecdote and before the woodcutter says he saw them. That his story and the woodcutter's agree means little since the priest actually saw nothing of the action that followed. However, it is presumed that the third-person recountings (the versions of the bandit, the wife, and the husband) are to be accepted as substantially true because in the court-scenes we see the woodcutter and the priest kneeling in the background and listening. Thus, they have been there to hear what the three have said, and if there were any differences in this third-person version they give the commoner, one might be expected to contradict the other. This, however, must be inferred by the viewer and, given the character of the priest, it is not at all certain that he is the kind of person who would contradict even if he saw that the stories were being falsified by the woodcutter in the re-telling.

To say this, however, is to presume that it is the woodcutter who is doing the re-telling and this is by no means certain. It could be equally well be the priest who is recounting—or it could be both of them. Since these three stories are mutually contradictory (or at least seem to be) we are initially given the choice of disbelieving the priest and the woodcutter, or disbelieving one and/or all of the original triangle of bandit, husband, wife.

Kurosawa gives us no reason at all for disbelieving the priest. At the same time we are given very little for disbelieving what is said by any of the original three because their stories, if lies, are not the kind of lies which one tells to escape punishment, and this would seem to be the usual reason for lying. The bandit admits to killing the husband; the wife admits to killing the husband; the husband admits to killing himself. There is no shifting of blame. Each pleads guilty.

There is, on the other hand, a reason for the woodcutter's lying. He is the only person who has something to gain from falsehood. First, as he says, he did not want to become involved with the police; second, it transpires that he might be a thief (the dagger) as well. One might understand his lying to keep clear of the police but under the gate with an all-forgiving priest and the kind of man who steals clothes from abandoned infants there seems little motivation for falsehood. If he stole the dagger the other two could not care less—though the commoner might covet it.

It would seem that someone—more than one—is lying. Yet there is no reason. At this point the thought occurs: is it not possible that no one is lying and that the stories can be reconciled?

The disagreement in the stories is only over the murder. All the stories of attack and rape agree. Kurosawa helps us very little in sorting out the different versions and their possible agreement, but he does help some. The bandit, for example, says that he and the husband fought because the wife insisted and, at the end of his version, he backs the husband into a thicket and kills him. The woodcutter agrees with the bandit: they fought because she insisted. At the end of his version, Kurosawa is careful to show us that it is the same thicket into which the husband is backed and killed. There are many differences (emotion, intention) but the actions in the first and fourth versions agree.

The problem is in reconciling the other two. The third version, that of the husband, may be hastily disposed of. He is dead. The dead do not speak—through the mouths of mediums or otherwise. That the three under the gate happen to believe in spirits does not mean that we must. Rape, murder, these are physical facts; the talking-dead are not. The poor, demented woman called upon by the magistrates, obviously terrified by her position, makes up her own version which (though she may believe it) is not, *cannot* be true. (That one need not be so cavalier with both an important section of the film and Kurosawa's express intentions will be demonstrated later: there is perfectly good reason for believing in both the speaking-dead and the veracity of the husband.)

This leaves the story of the wife. Hers is more difficult to reconcile but not impossible (if you cheat a bit). Apparently, after the rape, there was a lapse of some time—recounted in the woodcutter's story as well—when the bandit was not there. During this time her husband shows her how he has come to hate her. (This point is agreed upon in all the stories—leaving out the husband's which we, for the present, have agreed is no story at all. The implication in both the woodcutter's and the bandit's version is that it was the wife who suggested the duel, and so some amount of hate between the spouses is necessary.) She remembers that he looked at her with the greatest scorn. She cuts his bonds, offers him her dagger, asks him to kill her, then faints. When she revives, her husband is dead and the dagger is in his chest.

Now, if only it were not for the dagger, all the stories would more or less agree because she could just as easily have either fainted or lost her reason during a duel which followed and of which she would have known nothing. However, the dagger remains (as well as a number of other loose ends). Further, at the end of the film it transpires that the woodcutter might have taken it. He has now a very good reason for lying. Not only may he have stolen the dagger, he might also have crept up during the wife's swoon and stabbed the husband himself. Leaving aside the extreme unlikelihood of a simple woodcutter daring to stab a noble, however, what would have been the motivation for such an act? Robbery? But then a number of the couple's belongings would be missing and the police do not mention this and nor does the wife. The only missing objects are the horse and sword (which the bandit took) and the dagger (which the woodcutter might have taken). But, let us presume this is what happened—that either the wife or the woodcutter killed the husband.

One can do this because the woodcutter now has a reason for lying (possible murder) and this makes his story (both parts of it) falsehood. Then one remembers that his version happened to jibe particularly well with that of the bandit.

Where is the bandit now? His head has probably been cut off. At any rate he can tell us no more than the husband could. And who told us the bandit's story? Why the woodcutter, of course. And he lied about it, even taking care that it match and thus lend credulity to his own. If he has been the one who has told us all these stories, then they are all lies. But, in that case, why include two (husband's and wife's) that would weaken his own case? Perhaps it is because the priest tells these and the priest (though he has perhaps heard the bandit's story) does not presume to correct. Then, one solution to the "Great Rashomon Murder Mystery" would be:

1. The discovery of the husband's body.		A lie told by the woodcutter.
2. Husband and wife seen in the forest.		The truth told by the priest.
3. The bandit's capture.	Told by the police agent.	The truth told by the woodcutter or the priest.
4. The bandit's version of the story.	Told by the bandit.	A lie told by the woodcutter.
5. The wife's version.	Told by the wife.	The truth told by the priest.
6. The husband's version.	Told by the husband through the medium.	Accepted as true and told by the priest.
7. The woodcutter's version.		A lie told by the woodcutter.

There is some (not much) reason for the validity of this arrangement given in the context of the film itself. At the end of 4, the commoner is speaking to the woodcutter—as though he were responding to something which the woodcutter had told him. He says that he thinks the bandit Tajomaru probably killed the woman as well.

PRIEST: But the woman turned up in prison too, you know. It seems she went to seek refuge at some temple and the police found her there. . . .

WOODCUTTER: It's a lie. They're all lies. Tajomaru's confession, the woman's story—they're lies.

COMMONER: Well, men are only men. That's why they lie. They can't tell the truth, not even to themselves.

PRIEST: That may be true. But it's because men are so weak. That's why they lie. That's why they must deceive themselves.

COMMONER: Not another sermon! I don't mind a lie. Not if it's interesting. What kind of story did she tell?

PRIEST: Hers was a completely different story from the bandit's. Everything was different. Tajomaru talked about her temper. I saw nothing like that at all. I found her very pitiful. I felt great compassion for her.

Then follows the wife's version which, in this context, seems very much as though retold by the priest who, having no reason for lying, would himself tell the truth as he heard it.

It would be convenient if, at the end of 5, the woodcutter would have again said it was a lie but he unfortunately does not. He says nothing, merely states that the next story, the husband's story, is a lie. There is here no indication as to who tells 6 because the last word before it begins belongs to the commoner. Besides, at that moment (perhaps to prepare for the supernatural to come) there is a great flash of lightning, followed by thunder. At the end of 6, the woodcutter is walking about and then stops and says that it wasn't true. If he had been telling the dead husband's story he would not have said this. It must have been the priest. He goes on to say that it wasn't a dagger that killed him anyway. It was a sword. Now, we know that the bandit stole and sold the sword, but we do not actually know how the husband was killed. The woodcutter is telling us. Since he has lied about the dagger there is no reason to believe his remark about the sword. And it is here that the priest decides he doesn't want to hear any more—almost as though he can no longer countenance such lying from the woodcutter. It is now revealed that his having said he found the body was a lie and even the commoner becomes suspicious. At the end of 7:

COMMONER: And I suppose that is supposed to be true.

WOODCUTTER (*getting to his feet*): I don't tell lies. I saw it with my own eyes.

COMMONER: That I doubt.

WOODCUTTER: I don't tell lies.

COMMONER: Well, so far as that goes, no one tells lies after he has said that he is going to tell one.

PRIEST: But it's horrible—if men do not tell the truth, do not trust one another, then the earth becomes a kind of hell.

COMMONER: You are right. The world we live in is a hell.

It might be assumed then that the woodcutter is consistently lying, that the priest knows it but for some reason (fear, compassion) restrains himself. Therefore the only correct version is the woman's—which is given by the priest. Further, the woodcutter may have murdered the husband as well. The commoner says: "And you say you don't lie! That's just funny. Look, you may have fooled the police, but you don't fool me." Then the woodcutter attacks the commoner—perhaps not the act of an innocent man—and the two fight. Then:

PRIEST (*seeing the woodcutter pick up the baby and misinterpreting his intentions*): What are you trying to do? Take away what little it has left?

WOODCUTTER: I have six children of my own. One more wouldn't make it any more difficult.

PRIEST: I'm sorry. I shouldn't have said that.

WOODCUTTER: Oh, you can't afford not to be suspicious of people these days. I'm the one who ought to be ashamed. I don't know why I did a thing like that.

A thing like what? Is he confessing, indicating his guilt to this priest who refused to expose his lies in front of the commoner? Is this a kind of covenant between the two? Then this final gesture, the saving of the baby, might be a mark of contrition. The woodcutter will save a life and make amends either for the life he himself took or else did not prevent the wife from taking. And if this is true the final dialogue in the film is double-edged and profoundly ironic.

PRIEST: No, I am grateful to you. Because, thanks to you, I think I will be able to keep my faith in men.

But what if it were the priest that had told Tajomaru's story? What then? Well—what then indeed? The question, like this murder-mystery aspect of the film, is really irrelevant. It is only meaningful if one thinks that the picture is about relative truth. And if that were what it is about, would not Kurosawa have made the stories a bit less reconcilable than they are? If the film is about relative truth (which on one level it is, to be sure) then it is also a partial failure because, judging merely by externals—who did what to whom—the actions are not enough at variance to make a point which one might suppose that he (like Akutagawa) was making.

One doubts very much that Kurosawa was deeply interested in objective truth in this or in any other film. This is because the *why* is always implied. And in none of his pictures is Kurosawa even slightly interested in the why of a matter.

Instead, always, *how*. This offers a clue. The level of objective truth is not the truly interesting one. Much more interesting is the level of subjective truth. If the truth searched for becomes subjective, then no one lies, and the stories are wildly at variance.

Truth as it appears to others. This is one of the themes, perhaps the main one of this picture. No one—priest, woodcutter, husband, bandit, medium—lied. They all told the story the way they saw it, the way they believed it, and they all told the truth. Kurosawa therefore does not question truth. He questions reality.

Once asked why he thought that *Rashomon* had become so popular, both in Japan and abroad, he answered: "Well, you see . . . it's about this rape." Everyone laughed but the answer is not, perhaps, so cynical as it sounds. *Rashomon* is *about* an action as few pictures are *about* anything at all. We can turn the object this way and that, look at it from various angles, and it resembles a number of things but *is* only one thing—the object that it is. The film is about a rape (and a murder) but, more than this, it is about the reality of these events. Precisely, it is about what five people think this reality consists of. How an incident happens may reflect nothing about the incident itself but it must reflect something about the person involved in the happening and supplying the how.

Five people interpret an action and each interpretation is different because, in the telling and in the retelling, the people reveal not the action but themselves. This is why Kurosawa could leave the plot, insofar as there is one, dangling and unresolved. The fact that it *is* unresolved is itself one of the meanings of the film.

In all of Kurosawa's pictures there is this preoccupation with the conflict between illusion (the reactions of the five and their stories) and reality (the fact of the rape and murder). To do something is to realize that it is far different from what one had thought. To have done something and then to explain it completes the cycle because this too is (equally) different from what the thing itself was. Given a traumatic experience, one fraught with emotional connotations (murder, falling in love, bankruptcy, rape), reality escapes even more swiftly.

One can now assign various reasons for the five having seen and heard the things that they thought they saw and heard. All the stories have in common one single element—pride. Tajomaru is proud to have raped and fought and killed; the wife is proud to have (perhaps) killed; the husband (for now there is every reason to believe that the dead talk) is proud to have killed himself; and the woodcutter is proud to have seen and robbed. They are proud of these actions and we know because they insist upon them. One confesses only what one is openly or secretly proud of, which is the reason that contrition is rarely sincere. But the reasons for the pride, as Parker Tyler has indicated in his analysis of this film, are not those commonly encountered.[3]

Each is proud of what he did because, as he might tell you: "It is just the sort of thing that I would do." Each thinks of his character as being fully formed, of being a *thing,* like the rape or the dagger is a thing, and of his therefore (during an emergency such as this) being capable of only a certain number of (consistent) reactions. They are *in character* because they have defined their own character for themselves and will admit none of the surprising opportunities which must occur when one does not. They "had no choice"; circumstances "forced" their various actions; what each did "could not be helped." It is no wonder that the reported actions refuse to agree with each other. As the commoner has wisely remarked: "Men are only men . . . they can't tell the truth, not even to themselves." One of the points of the picture then is not that men will not but that men *cannot* tell the truth. The priest sees this: "It's because men are so weak. That's why they lie. That's why they must deceive themselves."

If one is going to agree that one is a certain kind of person one also agrees that one is engaged in self-deception, in bad faith. We know what Kurosawa thinks about this. From *Sugata Sanshiro* on, his villains have been in bad faith; that is, they see themselves as a kind of person to whom only certain actions, certain alternatives are open. In the effort to create themselves they only codify; in the effort to free themselves (by making action simpler and therefore easier) they limit themselves.

It is interesting that *Rashomon* should have been a historical film—Kurosawa's second (since the Japanese tend to think of the Meiji period—the era of *Sugata Sanshiro*—as being somehow modern),[4] because this limitation of spirit, this tacit agreement (social in its scope) that one *is* and cannot *become,* is a feudalistic precept which plagues the country to this day. This was as useful to the Kamakura Government as it proved to the administration during the last war. In

3. Tyler, "*Rashomon* as Modern Art," included in this volume.
4. The Meiji period (or "Meiji Restoration"), under the reign of the Emperor Mutsuhito, lasted from 1867 to 1912 and was the age of the great intensification of Japan's contact with the rest of the world. The Heian period, mentioned below, began with the removal of the capital from Nara to Heian (now Kyoto) in 784 and lasted about four centuries; nurtured by the culture of China, it was the age of the great flowering of Japanese civilization. *Rashomon* is presumably set in the decaying last years of the Heian period, as emblematized by the condition of the once-splendid gate from which the film takes its title.

Rashomon, as in *They Who Step on the Tiger's Tail* and *Sanjuro,* Kurosawa is presenting an indictment of feudal remnants. That he sets the scene in the Heian period is perhaps due to Akutagawa's having used it, and where the director follows the author in this film, he does so literally. The people, and their way of thinking, however, are completely feudal.

Rashomon is like a vast distorting mirror or, better, a collection of prisms that reflect and refract reality. By showing us its various interpretations (perhaps the husband really loved his wife, was lost without her and hence felt he must kill himself; perhaps she really thought to save her husband by a show of affection for the bandit, and thus played the role of faithful wife; perhaps the woodcutter knows much more, perhaps he too entered the action—mirrors within mirrors, each intention bringing forth another, until the triangle fades into the distance) he has shown first, that human beings are incapable of judging reality, much less truth, and, second, that they must continually deceive themselves if they are to remain true to the ideas of themselves that they have.

Here then, more than in any other single film, is found Kurosawa's central theme: the world is illusion, you yourself make reality, but this reality undoes you if you submit to being limited by what you have made. The important corollary—you are not, however, truly subject to this reality, you can break free from it, can live even closer to the nature you are continually creating—occurs only in the later films.

The visual starting point remains the Akutagawa stories. The author's description of the gate and medieval Kyoto is literally followed by both the script and camera. There is, for example, no reason at all for the bandit to be discovered by the police agent near a small bridge (seen in the film) except that this is where Akutagawa says it happened. What turned out to be an excellent cinematic device, all the testimonies being given to the audience, questions answered by unheard questions being repeated as a question and then answered by those testifying, is taken directly from the author. Likewise, in the original script, all the characters' names are retained even though, in the case of husband and wife, they never appear in the dialogue. Given the eventual difference between story and film—which is extreme and which the Japanese critics complained of when they said the director had been false to the spirit of the tales—such literal fidelity is remarkable.

The acting style, however, owes nothing at all to Akutagawa or any of his suggestions. It springs from a different source. "We were staying in Kyoto," says

Kurosawa, "waiting for the set to be finished. While we were there we ran off some 16 mm. prints to amuse ourselves. One of them was a Martin Johnson jungle film in which there was a shot of a lion roaming around. I noticed it and told Mifune that that was just what I wanted him to be. At the same time Mori had seen a jungle picture in which a black leopard was shown. We all went to see it. When the leopard came on Machiko was so upset that she hid her face. I saw and recognized the gesture. It was just what I wanted for the young wife."

Cinematically, the style is made of various parts, all of which work admirably together. Perhaps the most noticeable is a kind of rhapsodic impressionism which carries the story and creates the atmosphere. Take, for example, the much-admired walk of the woodcutter through the forest. This is cinematic impressionism—one literally receives impressions: the passing trees overhead, the sun, the glint of sunlight on the ax. Again, during the rape scene, the camera seeks the sky, the sun, the trees, contrasting this with the two, wife and bandit. When the rape is consummated and just before we return to the prison courtyard for the conclusion of the bandit's story, the sun comes out from behind a branch, dazzling, shining directly into the lenses: a metaphor. Just as much a metaphor certainly as the scene shortly before where the wife drops her dagger and it falls point first to land upright, quivering in the ground; or the celebrated scene where the bandit is asleep and the couple pass by. He has mentioned the breeze in his testimony. Now we see it (accompanied by the cooling celesta on the sound track) as it ruffles his hair. He opens his eyes and sees it raising the woman's veil. It is an extended metaphor, like a two-line poem.

Kurosawa in this film, and more than in any other, makes use of contrasting shots. A shot of the woman is held for a certain length of time. This is matched by a shot of the bandit, held for the same time. He intercuts these, back and forth, matching the timing so delicately that one does not notice the number of repeats while watching the film—and is surprised upon reading the script to discover that there are so many.

In the same way he uses single close-ups to emphasize the triangular nature of the story. A shot of the woman is followed by a shot of the bandit, followed by a shot of the husband, and this process continues, going round and round as it were. Mostly, however, he insists upon the triangle through composition. The picture is filled with masterful triangular compositions, often one following directly after another, the frame filled with woman, bandit, husband, but always in different compositional relationships to each other. When the Japanese critics mentioned Kurosawa's "silent-film technique" they meant his great reliance upon composition—which with this film became, and still remains, one of the strongest elements of the director's film style.

Kurosawa's use of cinematic punctuation is always imaginative and he is one of the few directors remaining who can intelligently use that most maligned of punctuation marks: the wipe. There is a fine use of it when the woman is waiting, during the bandit's story, and it (as always with Kurosawa) gives the effect of time, usually a short period of time, having elapsed.

Kurosawa does not usually use fades (either in or out), tending to be suspicious of the softening effect they produce. Certainly the ending of *The Lower Depths*— it ends on an unexpected cut—would be far less effective with a fade-out. He uses it only, as in the opening and closing of *The Throne of Blood,* when he deliberately wants the effect of distance and uninvolvement. For Kurosawa the fade usually means the elegiac.

The dissolve in his films, on the other hand, usually means time passing. The end of *Rashomon* is a beautiful example of this. The three men are standing under the gate and there is a series of dissolves moving closer and closer. This is almost a rhetorical device since, in actuality, not much time could have passed. It is a formal gesture, a gesture which makes us look, and makes us feel. If the purpose is merely to indicate passage of time, however, Kurosawa has even simpler ways of doing it—one of the most imaginative in this picture is where the husband is waiting and his voice tells us that he waited a very long time. Here the effect is given through three long-held shots with no dissolves or wipes at all—simply a long-shot, followed by a far-shot, followed by a medium close-up. These are used so consummately that one does not question that hours have passed.

Kurosawa's preoccupation with time (*the* preoccupation for any serious director) began with *Rashomon*. There are two kinds of time which concern him— and any other director. One is ostensible time—the time the story takes. The other is a certain kind of psychological time, the time that each sequence, and that each shot within this sequence takes. The first kind is the kind which is appreciable to the audience as well. *Rashomon* is a series of flashbacks, all of them both true and false; *Ikiru* on the other hand is a film in which flashback leads into further flashback—the scene where the father finds the baseball bat, remembers the ballgame, remembers the operation, remembers the hospital, remembers the son going off to war. The second half of *Ikiru* is a series of flash-

backs, in the *Citizen Kane* manner (a film which Kurosawa had not yet seen), which reconstructs the hero's life. The second kind of time is the kind of which no audience is aware—this is created in the alchemy of the cutting room.

In *Rashomon* one remembers a series of seemingly actual, or at least realistic, actions. And yet the film—extraordinarily so, even for Kurosawa—is a mosaic. The average of the shorter cuts is 2 ft. (1⅓ seconds) and, though there are several shorter cuts, and though scenes also last for minutes (the dialogue scenes under the gate), still, the average length of each shot is shorter in *Rashomon* than in any other of Kurosawa's films. This always has the effect of reality on the screen. As Naoki Noborikawa has noticed: "In *Rashomon* there is a scene where Tajomaru takes Takehiro [the husband] into the woods, then runs back and tells the woman that her husband has been bitten by a snake. The scenery through which the two together run to where he has left the husband tied up, is full of great natural beauty but the camera passes by it in one flash. I had thought that this was one shot, a swiftly moving pan. Seeing the film for the second time, however, I noticed that this was not so, and when I counted, on seeing it for the third time, I was surprised to discover that there were seven cuts in this small scene." As Kurosawa knew full well, one cuts fast and often for fast sections, slow and seldom for slow. But another reason for the extreme brevity of the *Rashomon* shots might be that the director knew he was asking his audience to look at the same material four or more times. He could not rely upon the novelty of the pictorial image to help sustain interest.

In addition, and maybe for the same reasons, he probably never moved the camera more than in *Rashomon*. The shooting script is full of directions to pan, to dolly in and out, etc. He used a favorite device of a dolly shot directly attached to a pan shot to get a continuity of action, and he was unusually careful of action continuity. This great mobility never calls attention to itself but gives the effect of continuous movement which we remember as being part of the style of the film.

All of these shots, stationary or moving, are calculated as to their time on the screen and their effect there. There are few other directors who know so precisely the proper length for a given section of film. The shot of the dog carrying the human hand at the opening of *Yojimbo* is an example. One second less and we would not have known what he was carrying; one second more and the scene would have been forced, vulgar. In *Rashomon* the dagger drops into the ground and is allowed to quiver just twice. All of the images are handled in this imaginative and economical manner. Kurosawa rarely makes a mistake in his timing, and the inner or psychological timing of *Rashomon* is perfection. There are 407 separate shots in the body of the film (with 10 more for titles making a total of 417). This is more than twice the number in the usual film, and yet these shots never call attention to themselves—rather, they make it possible for us to feel this film, to be reached with immediacy, to be drawn into it, intellectually curious and emotionally aware. In a very special way, *Rashomon*—like any fine film—creates within its audience the very demand which it satisfies.

For a director as young as Kurosawa—he was then forty—and particularly for so young a Japanese director, the film is remarkably free from influences. Though some scenes owe something to Dovshenko's *Aerograd,* they owe nothing at all to Fritz Lang's *Siegfried* (an ostensible "influence" often mentioned) because the director had never seen it. The structure may owe something to *The Marriage Circle,* that Lubitsch film which Kurosawa—like most Japanese directors—remembers with affection and admiration, but the debt is very slight.

Of the style, Kurosawa has said only: "I like silent pictures and I always have. They are often so much more beautiful than sound pictures are. Perhaps they had to be. At any rate, I wanted to restore some of this beauty. I thought of it, I remember, in this way: one of the techniques of modern art is simplification, and that I must therefore simplify this film." Simplification is also one of the techniques of Japanese art and long has been. Those who noticed a "Japanese" look about some of the scenes (mainly their composition, aside from temple architecture, sand gardens and the like) were right, though the director had perhaps achieved this through his own knowledge of simplified painting techniques in the West—those of Klee and Matisse for example. Otherwise there is little "Japanese" influence. In fact the film is the complete opposite of the ordinary Japanese historical film in that it questions while they reaffirm; it is realistic, while they are romantic; it is using its period as a pretext and a decoration while the ordinary period film aims at simple reconstruction. Despite foreign commentary on the subject, there is no influence from classical Japanese drama. Only the sword-fighting techniques owe something to the modern Japanese stage. Anyone who has ever seen Kabuki will realize the enormous difference between its acting style and that of *Rashomon.*[5] The acting in the film is naturalistic, in the Japanese sense of the word. It is apparently unrestrained, and it is in the grand manner which the West once knew but has now almost lost. Indeed, Mifune as the bandit was so "grand" that even Japanese critics complained of overacting. There is a

5. The actors of Japan's popular Kabuki theatre (established in the seventeenth century) are famous for their highly stylized gestural and vocal techniques.

debt to the stage, however, though the stage is Japanese modern theater—the Shingeki. Since the budget was small, the sets (there are only two—both studio sets—the gate and the prison courtyard) are deliberately stylized and simplified in the manner of modern stage scenery (again, not Kabuki scenery, which is flamboyant, detailed, and very nineteenth century to the eye). Likewise, the costumes owe much to modern stage costumes, with their simplicity, their lack of ornament. The music also owes much to incidental-music methods of the modern Japanese stage.

That the music owes even more to another source is notorious and some Western critics have complained that the film was partially spoiled for them. This is not the fault of the composer. The late Fumio Hayasaka was one of Japan's most individual and creative composers and it was Kurosawa himself who said "write something like Ravel's *Boléro*"—a work which in Japan had not yet become as clichéd as in the West. The composer complied and the results, as a matter of fact, do detract—particularly from the opening scenes.

The shooting time for the film was unusually short (it was completed within a matter of weeks because most of the pre-production work had been done for some time) and it is one of the few Kurosawa pictures that did not go over its budget. Daiei, though loudly announcing that it had no idea what the picture was about, nevertheless exhibited it with some care. It was given a formal premiere in what was then one of Tokyo's best theaters; the press was invited and it had an initial run of two weeks (the usual run was only a single week) at all the theaters in the Daiei chain. Contrary to later legend, it was not a box office failure—it ranked fourth in Daiei's 1950 listings of best money-earners. Nor did the audience seem to have trouble understanding it.

Daiei, though more pleased than not with its second Kurosawa picture, made no attempt to detain him when he returned to Toho and, after the second and third runs were completed, shelved the picture. There it would probably have remained had it not been for a series of fortuitous circumstances which led to its becoming the best-known Japanese film ever made.

Venice sent an invitation to Japan asking that a film be entered in the film festival. This was before Japan became as well-acquainted with film festivals as it is now, and there was consternation as to what to send. *Rashomon* was not even considered. In the meantime, at the request of Venice, Guilliana Stramigioli, then head of Italiafilm in Japan, had viewed a number of Japanese films, had seen *Rashomon,* and had liked it. When she recommended it, however, the suggestion was met with much opposition—particularly from Daiei which had neither hope nor faith in the film. It was with the greatest reluctance that they agreed to send the film to the 1951 Venice Festival, where it won first prize.

Its winning what was then the best-thought-of cinema prize came as a profound shock to Japan. For one thing, it had not been made for export and there remains a long-standing Japanese prejudice that things not especially constructed for foreigners will not be understood by them. For another, the Japanese critics had not liked the film. Tadashi Iijima thought the film failed because of "its insufficient plan for visualizing the style of the original stories"; Tatsuhiko Shigeno objected to the language, saying that no robber would ever use words that big. Other critics thought the script was too complicated, or that the direction was too monotonous, or that there was too much cursing. What perhaps most surprised the Japanese, however, was that a historical film (and they continued to think of *Rashomon* as "historical" in the "costume-picture" sense of the word) should prove acceptable to the West. This eventually led to a rash of Western-aimed "historical" films—of which *Gate of Hell* is the only surviving example—but initially critics were at a loss to explain its winning the Venice prize and its consequent popularity in most other countries.[6] Eventually, they decided that it was because *Rashomon* was "exotic" (in the sense that *Gate of Hell* is truly exotic—and little else) and that foreigners like exoticism. Even now it is the rare critic who will admit that *Rashomon* could have had any other appeal to the West.

Once the rare critic is found, however, he will say—as several have—that the reason the West liked it was because the reasoning in the picture was "Western," by which is meant analytic, logical, and speculative—processes which are indeed not often found in patterns of Japanese thought. Recognizing that the film questions reality yet champions hope, the critic says that this is not the Japanese way and, in a sense, he is right. Actually, of course, what had happened is that in this film (though not for the first time in Japanese cinema history) the confines of "Japanese" thought could not contain the director, who thereby joined the world at large. *Rashomon* speaks to everyone, not just to the Japanese.

Kurosawa has said: "Japanese are terribly critical of Japanese films, so it is not too surprising that a foreigner should have been responsible for my film's being sent to Venice. It was the same way with Japanese woodcuts—it was the for-

---

6. Noted especially for its use of color, *Gate of Hell* (1953, directed by Teinosuke Kinugasa) was, along with *Rashomon*, one of the films primarily responsible for awakening the Western movie-going public to Japanese cinema.

eigners who first appreciated them. We Japanese think too little of our own things. Actually, *Rashomon* wasn't all that good, I don't think. Yet, when people have said to me that its reception was just a stroke of luck, a fluke, I have answered by saying that they only say these things because the film is, after all, Japanese, and then I wonder: Why do we all think so little of our own things? Why don't we stand up for our films? What are we so afraid of?''

Though Daiei did not retain the director, it followed the usual maxim of film companies: if you have a success, repeat it. In the following year Daiei's Keigo Kimura made *The Beauty and the Bandits* which was taken directly from *Rashomon,* and the much better *Tale of Genji* by Kimisaburo Yoshimura. Kurosawa himself, his reputation enormously enhanced by the international success of the film, went back to Toho to make *Ikiru.* Show-biz decided that Japan had made an unexampled breakthrough into the "foreign market," and the man on the street was as delighted over the Venice prize as he would have been had a Japanese athlete won an Olympic medal. Thus, in a way, the worth of *Rashomon* was partially obscured by its own success. It is only now that one realizes it is one of the few living films from Japan's cinematic past. Its frequent revivals in Japan, its frequent re-showings in other countries, its constant appearance in retrospectives, the fact that it is still talked about, still discussed, makes one finally realize that, along with *Ikiru* and *Seven Samurai,* it is a masterpiece.

Kurosawa

His Life and Art

Audie E. Bock

Searching for the sources of Akira Kurosawa's inspirations, more than one Japanese film critic has come to the conclusion that this screenwriter-director's point of departure lies in his own personal situation. Some flatly assert that he always makes films about himself. A note of corroboration for this approach lies in a suggestion from his line producer and script girl since 1950, Teruyo Nogami, who feels that one of the motivations behind the story line of his 1980 film *Kagemusha: The Shadow Warrior* was his perception that he has no artistic successor, and no one to act as his double, in the Japanese film world. These deductions offered by those close to Kurosawa as well as those who study him through the screen from afar seem to lend credence to the notion that there exists a link between his personal life and the choice of subjects and themes in his work.

The director himself vehemently denies any such link, with one sole exception. He has described his 1952 film *Ikiru* as arising from thoughts about what he himself would do and feel if faced with the same sudden ultimatum as its hero: a maximum of six months to live before terminal cancer removes all possibilities for action. Yet Kurosawa has never in actuality confronted a fatal disease, and in fact he conceived and filmed *Ikiru* at a time when he was unquestionably in his physical and productive prime, at the age of forty-one. As evidence, in his forthcoming autobiography he speaks of the circumstances surrounding the shooting

This essay first appeared in the program of the Kurosawa retrospective sponsored by the Japan Film Center, a unit of the Japan Society, at Japan House, New York, from 9 October to 20 October, 1981.

of his 1950 film *Rashomon* with great nostalgia for the youthful energy that he and his cast and crew shared at that point in their lives.[1]

But because the writer-director himself denies a relationship between his life and his work, it becomes necessary to examine his personal history to evaluate this contradiction. Akira Kurosawa was born in Tokyo on March 23, 1910. His father was a native of Akita Prefecture, in the deep north, with a lineage going back to one of the most famous samurai of northern Japan, Abe Sadato (1015– 1062), who led an ill-fated war against Minamoto Yoriyoshi of the powerful Genji clan. Kurosawa's mother's family, on the other hand, had their origins in Osaka merchant culture. Aside from several hearty outdoor summers spent with relatives in the Akita countryside, Kurosawa grew up and received all of his education in Tokyo. His father was a physical-education teacher and administrator at the Toyama Army Academy, and his mother a career housewife who raised eight children, of which Akira was the youngest.

Among the formative influences Kurosawa has cited in his childhood are his father's love of the movies, his older brother's love of Russian literature and career choice as a silent film narrator, and some of his grade-school teachers' encouragement in sports and painting (he also took *kendo* fencing lessons as a child, inspired by a demonstration given at school). His most painful experiences included the Great Kanto Earthquake of 1923, his brother's suicide as a young man, the death from illness of the older sister closest to him, and to a lesser extent the discovery that he could not make a living as a painter and member of the Proletarian Artists' League during the Depression, when he also participated in underground political activities.

Once Kurosawa became an employee of a film production company, by application, he went through the usual six-year apprenticeship before making his first film, the 1943 *Sugata Sanshiro*. He attributes a great deal of the skills he acquired to a patient, encouraging and responsive teacher, director Kajiro Yamamoto, who was a prolific maker of both comedies and action dramas.

During the war era, Kurosawa suffered bitterly from the constraints of censorship, but he never gave up the hope of making good films, as did some who refused to change their established style and were content to comply with national policy directives. Toward the end of the war, while Tokyo was being bombed, Kurosawa married the woman who had starred in his second film, *The Most Beautiful*, Yoko Yaguchi, who became a housewife and mother of his two children.

---

1. Subsequently published as *Something Like an Autobiography,* trans. Audie E. Bock (New York: Alfred A. Knopf, 1982). See "An Autobiographical Account" in this volume.

The postwar era brought a new freedom to treat contemporary life in film, but also a bitter struggle between workers and management in the Toho film production company. The dismissals and resignations that occured as a result of a series of strikes separated Kurosawa from some of his closest colleagues. These events account for his having become a freelance director and making five films with companies other than Toho between 1949 and 1951. By this time he had won the Venice International Film Festival's Golden Lion for *Rashomon* and become a director of world renown.

Since the early fifties Kurosawa has been involved in making movies above all else. He has frequently, if reluctantly, traveled abroad, and as the Japanese film industry began its decline in the late sixties accepted an offer to direct the Japanese side of a Twentieth Century Fox production, *Tora Tora Tora.* Cross-cultural communication, financial and artistic control problems and the allegation that he was mentally unsound led to his resignation from the project.

The adverse publicity surrounding the 1968 *Tora Tora Tora* incident proved extremely damaging to Kurosawa's career. He was unable to get major financing for his projects and ended by making *Dodeskaden* in 1970 as a low-budget independent production with his friends, directors Keisuke Kinoshita, Masaki Kobayashi and Kon Ichikawa, as co-producers. This attempt to prove that he was not insane and was capable of making a movie with a small amount of money (filmed in 28 days) emerged as an interesting experiment in color and storytelling method, but it was his first commercial failure. Despondency over these poor results, combined with the physical discomfort of an undiagnosed case of serious gallstones led him to attempt suicide.

Upon recovery he happily accepted an offer from the U.S.S.R. to film a project of his choice on Soviet soil. After two years of shooting under extreme conditions of heat and cold in Siberia, *Dersu Uzala,* the 1976 Academy Award winner for Best Foreign Language Film was the result. Another outcome, less fortuitous, was chronic poor circulation in the director's feet, the aftermath of frostbite.

In the spare moments when not writing or directing a film Kurosawa reads widely in everything from classics of world and Japanese literaure to American detective novels. He plays golf, but otherwise eschews much social activity, preferring to spend time with his family, his grandchildren in particular. Although his status as an international film figure sends him to foreign countries periodically, he would rather travel no farther than his summer house on a golf course near Mount Fuji, unless he is scouting locations for a film.

The above account illustrates a contrast between a director like Kurosawa and one for whom life and art are very much intertwined, like the late Kenji Mizoguchi, who made film after film about the women he both idealized and feared. There is little in Kurosawa's personal history to trigger associations with his film story lines. With the exception of the painful experiences cited in Kurosawa's youth, there appear to be few incidents of a sensational value in his life to compare with the Mizoguchi who was stabbed by an irate sweetheart and suffered the pain of watching his wife go insane from syphilis. It is almost as if Kurosawa keeps his personal life as removed as possible from his work in order to allow his artistic imagination a freer rein. He has never dwelt on a personal experience in his films—there are no earthquake movies, no strike movies (he disclaims authorship of a strike-movie sequence Toho has always attributed to him), no Felliniesque films about film directors' private agonies. Certainly Kurosawa's life has not lacked high adventure, intense emotion, and moments of extreme pathos and humor, but when these dramatic elements emerge on the screen they appear to come from other source material.

Kurosawa asserts that he has never made an "assigned" film. He writes all of his own scripts, based on his own ideas. He feels that this is the only way to retain full artistic control of the material. Yet he does not claim that every idea for every film he has made emerged exclusively from his own imagination. (He has done enough literary and theatrical adaptations not to make a point of exclusively original scripts.) He places a high value on the catalytic input from diverse sources. When he decided he wanted to make a period film subsequent to *Ikiru,* for example, he recalls that producer Shojiro Motoki one day suggested the title "Seven Samurai," and the whole structure of the story blossomed from this free-floating title, attached to no form at the time it was uttered.

In spite of the denial of real-life connections to film concepts, there have been instances of characters from Kurosawa's own experience intruding on his films. Also in his autobiography, he recalls a realization that came upon him after developing the character of Hiruta, the shabby laywer in *Scandal* (1950). The real-life model for the guilt-ridden alcoholic with a sick but angelic daughter had emerged from a memory of Kurosawa's days as an assistant director, frequenting the bars near the studio. The tapping of real life, however, was unconscious, and recognized only long after the fact. Kurosawa brings it up not as a defense for his inspiration, but as an example of the inevitable impingement of reality upon fiction. "The character wrote himself," he marvels, "I had no control over the pen."

The most cogent argument against the interpretation of Kurosawa's films as an expression of or elaboration upon his own life emerges from his method of screenwriting. He has never written a script without the collaboration of at least one person, and in some cases as many as four. The writing team of Kurosawa, Shinobu Hashimoto, and Hideo Oguni produced a number of Japan's classic films of the fifties and sixties, including *Seven Samurai.* The system of proposing ideas and characters, sharing criticisms as well as inspirations, and hashing through the plausibility of motivations and dialogue from start to finish prevents any one contributor's idea from becoming so personal as to lose the audience. The division of input is difficult to determine in the way credits appear on the screen in the finished film—the method has consisted of many inn rooms filled with crumpled pieces of paper, the rejected ideas removed without record. But Kurosawa has described Oguni as the humanistic "heart" of the team, while Hashimoto has been the "brain" technician of plot. And he has credited his most recent collaborator, Masato Ide, with some of the great moments of screen time. The critical scene with the ladies in *Kagemusha,* for example, succeeds because of Ide's suggestion to have the double confess to them that he is an impostor, and find his confession treated as a joke.

Other factors too have influenced the conception of Kurosawa's stories, among them the planning of particular roles for particular actors. To illustrate the development of a script altered by the personality of an actor, Kurosawa has cited *Drunken Angel,* in which Toshiro Mifune's character, the gangster, took away central-figure status from the doctor played by Takashi Shimura. This was a case where the electrifying energy of Mifune as a young man proved impossible to tone down even in the writing phase of the film's preparation.

The end result has been a number of films that set the standard for entertainment and inspiration in today's cinema. Battles of great medieval clans and scruffy, masterless samurai with peasants come from someone who has never been at war. Superhero unshaven warriors and slowly-awakening bureaucrats come from someone who has never been either. Gangsters and physicians, young factory girls proving their worth as workers and patriots, rape, murder, betrayal, ransom all come from the imagination of a man who has not experienced these things in his own life. But if they are lacking in his life, few would say his films have suffered as a result.

Kurosawa frequently begs out of making statements to the public by saying, "Everything I have to say is on the screen; a filmmaker should not step out in front of it and talk about his work." He likewise avoids discussion of his personal life, but presumably what he has to say on the screen includes his reactions to the large events of his private life, translated into the universal medium of a good film story so that they can have meaning for other people as well. The making of an eloquent cinematic statement does not necessarily require the writer-director to treat his own life on the screen; it does, however, require him to treat situations and characters about which both he and an audience can care deeply, and which in so doing embody thoughtful reflections on his own life.[2]

2. Since this essay was written, Kurosawa has completed one more film, *Ran*. See "Filmography" in this volume.

Rashomon

Rashomon

When the editor once asked Akira Kurosawa about the meaning of a scene, the director replied, "If I could have said it in words, I wouldn't have gone to the trouble and expense of making a film." Paradoxically, with very minor exceptions the final text of *Rashomon* is almost identical to the script that Kurosawa and his long-time collaborator, Shinobu Hashimoto, had written before the filming began. Exceptions include additional shots, e.g., during the woodcutter's walk through the forest and during the fights between bandit and husband; in addition, slight revisions of dialogue were made, especially in the final sequence.

In this volume, camera position is indicated by initials:

CU	close-up
MCU	medium close-up
MS	medium shot
LS	long shot

Camera movement is indicated by the following:

pan	camera turning sideways while remaining fixed on its axis
tilt	camera moving up or down while fixed on its axis
dolly	camera moving toward or away from a fixed subject
track	camera moving at the same speed as the subject being filmed
travel	camera moving at a speed independent of a moving subject

Credits and Cast

The credits for the film are superimposed over the opening shots of a gate.

Director
Akira Kurosawa

Executive Producer
Masaichi Nagata

Producer
Jingo Minoru

Production Company
Daiei

Screenplay
Shinobu Hashimoto, Akira Kurosawa; based on two stories by Ryunosuke Akutagawa

Cinematography
Kazuo Miyagawa

Art Direction
So Matsuyama

Lighting
Kenichi Okamoto

Music
Fumio Hayasaka

Length
88 minutes

Release Date
August 25, 1950, Tokyo;
December 26, 1951, New York

U.S. Distributor
Initially, RKO, then Edward Harrison; now Janus Films

Tajomaru, the bandit
Toshiro Mifune

Takehiro, the samurai
Masayuki Mori

Masago, the wife
Machiko Kyo

The Woodcutter
Takashi Shimura

The Priest
Minoru Chiaki

The Commoner
Kichijiro Ueda

The Police Agent
Daisuke Kato

The Medium
Fumiko Honma

The Continuity Script

*The title sequence consists of some ten shots of the half-ruined gate,
Rashomon, in the rain. Superimposed over these are the title and credits,
including, in some prints distributed in the United States, vignettes (oval-
shaped insets) showing the major characters in action. Various details of
the gate are seen: its steps, the base of a column, the eaves of the roof,
puddles on the ground. Everywhere there is evidence of the downpour.*
Gagaku, *traditional court music, is heard during the credits, then the
sound of the torrential rain.*
*The final title reads: "Kyoto, in the twelfth century, when famines and
civil wars had devastated the ancient capital."* [1]

1. LS: *two men, a priest and a woodcutter, are sitting motionless, taking
   shelter under the gate.*

2. MS *from the side of the two, the woodcutter in the foreground, as they
   stare out at the rain with heads bowed. The woodcutter raises his head.*

   WOODCUTTER: I can't understand it. I just can't understand it at all.

3. MCU *of the priest; he looks at the woodcutter and back again at the rain.*

4. LS *from directly in front. The two men continue to stare vacantly at the
   rain.*

5. *A general* LS *view of the gate; a man enters from behind the camera and
   runs toward the gate, splashing through puddles. Thunder is heard.*

6. LS *from reverse angle. The man runs past a fallen column, and disappears from the frame.*

---

1. This title does not appear in all release prints. Note that Kurosawa here identifies the period as the
twelfth century, while elsewhere (see "An Autobiographical Account" in this volume) he speaks of
his "eleventh-century period film." Moreover, the essays in this volume by Sato, Tyler, and Davidson
suggest still different centuries. But the over-all mood of decadence and cynicism, as well as the
condition of the Rashomon gate itself, suggest that the film is set very late in the Heian period.

7. MS *of the steps of the gate; he enters from behind the camera and runs up the steps to shelter.*

8. MS: *out of the rain, he turns and looks back outside, then removes a rag covering his head and wrings it out. The woodcutter's voice is heard.*

   WOODCUTTER (*off-screen*): I just can't understand it.

9. LS: *the newcomer, in the background, turns toward the priest and wood-cutter, who are sitting in the foreground.*

10. MS *of the newcomer. He goes toward the others—the camera panning with him—and sits down behind the woodcutter.*

    COMMONER: What's the matter?

11. MS *of the woodcutter and commoner.*

    COMMONER: What can't you understand?
    WOODCUTTER: I've never heard of anything so strange.
    COMMONER: Why don't you tell me about it?

12. MS *of all three men, the priest in the foreground. The commoner looks toward the priest.*

    COMMONER: Good thing we have a priest here—he looks smart too.
    PRIEST: Oh, even Abbot Konin of the Kiyomizu Temple, though he's known for his learning, wouldn't be able to understand this.
    COMMONER: Then you know something about this story?
    PRIEST: I've heard it with my own ears, seen it with my own eyes. And only today.
    COMMONER: Where?
    PRIEST: In the prison courtyard.
    COMMONER: The prison?
    PRIEST: A man has been murdered.
    COMMONER: What of it? One or two more . . . (*He stands up.*)

13. MS *of the commoner standing over the others; he looks down.*

> COMMONER: Only one? Why, if you go up to the top of this gate you'll always find five or six bodies. Nobody bothers about them. *(He begins to take off his shirt.)*

14. MS *of the priest; he turns and looks up at the commoner.*

> PRIEST: Oh, you're right. Wars, earthquakes, great winds, fires, famines, plague—each new year is full of disaster. *(He wipes his hand across his face.)*

15. MS, *as in 13: the commoner wrings out his wet shirt.*

> PRIEST *(off-screen):* And now every night the bandits descend upon us.

16. MS *of the priest, as in 14.*

> PRIEST: I, for one, have seen hundreds of men dying, killed like animals. *(Pause.)* Yet . . . even I have never heard anything as horrible as this before.

17. MS *of the woodcutter, who has been listening; he turns to the priest.*

18. MS, *as in 14: the priest turns toward the woodcutter.*

19. MS *of the woodcutter and priest.*

> WOODCUTTER: Horrible—it's horrible.

The woodcutter looks away; dolly in to CU *of the priest.*

> PRIEST: There was never anything as terrible as this. Never. It is more horrible than fires or wars or epidemics—or bandits. *(Camera stays on him.)*
> COMMONER *(off-screen):* Look here now, priest—let's not have any sermons.

The priest looks up.

20. MS *of the commoner, as in 13.*

> COMMONER: I only wanted to know about this strange story of yours because it might amuse me while I wait out the rain. But I'd just as soon sit quietly and listen to the rain than hear any sermons from you. *(His wet shirt over his shoulder, he moves toward the camera.)*

21. LS: *the commoner moves away, leaving the priest and woodcutter sitting as before.*

22. MS *of the commoner at the other side of the gate; he peers at some loose boards, then rips two of them free.*

23. LS: *he crosses back to squat in front of the woodcutter and priest, and begins to pull the boards to pieces. The woodcutter rises and runs over to him.*

> WOODCUTTER: Maybe you can tell me what it all means. I don't understand it. *(He squats down.)* All three of them . . .
> COMMONER: All three of whom?
> WOODCUTTER: It's those three I wanted to tell you about.
> COMMONER: All right, tell me then, but don't get so excited. This rain won't let up for some time. *(Both men look up.)*

24. CU *of the great signboard of the gate, seen in the opening shot of the titles: the sign reads "Rashomon" in large Japanese characters. The camera tilts down from the signboard to the men far below. The woodcutter moves closer to the commoner.*

25. CU *of the woodcutter.*

> WOODCUTTER: It was three days ago. I'd gone into the mountains for wood . . .

26. *The dazzling light of the sun breaks through the branches of trees overhead as the camera travels through a dense woods. Music begins, a steady rhythm supporting a melody initially associated with the woodcutter but later becoming the underlying musical theme of the entire film.*

27. CU *of the woodcutter's ax, seen in a traveling shot, glinting in the sunlight as the woodcutter walks through the woods.*

28. MCU *of the woodcutter's face as he walks, ax over his shoulder, the camera tracking backward.*

29. LS: *panning from high above, the camera follows him.*

30. *A tree; the camera tilts from top to bottom to discover the woodcutter in the distance.*

31. *The camera pans with the woodcutter as he approaches a narrow bridge, crosses it, and goes off.*

32. *A forward-traveling shot of the sky seen through the branches of the trees passing overhead.*

33. MCU *of the woodcutter's back as he walks, the camera tracking after him.*

34. *A traveling shot as he moves rightward from* LS *closer to camera.*

35. *The sky and the tree branches, as in 32.*

36. *The camera travels toward the woodcutter, crosses in front of him, and pans around to follow his back receding into the woods.*

37. *The sun through the tree branches, as in 26.*

38. *The woodcutter from above. The camera travels as the woodcutter approaches, pans, and travels with him again, closer now, occasionally losing sight of him in the underbrush.*

39. *Extreme close-up of the back of the woodcutter's head, the camera tracking after him; again, the leaves sometimes block the view.*

40. ECU: *a traveling shot alongside the woodcutter; the view is frequently blocked.*

41. ECU *of the woodcutter's face as he walks toward the camera, camera tracking backward. Suddenly he and camera halt. Music ends.*

42. CU *of a woman's reed hat with veil, dangling on a branch near the ground. The woodcutter, in the background, looks at it and comes forward to touch the veil. Audible is a soft tinkle like the sound of wind chimes; it develops into bell-like music which is later associated with the woman. The woodcutter slowly walks on, the camera panning to watch as he recedes farther into the woods. The main thematic music begins again.*

43. MS: *traveling shot alongside the woodcutter; he looks about on either side as he walks cautiously on.*

44. *He approaches the camera and (*MCU*) looks down. He halts.*

45. *A close shot of a man's hat lying at his feet; he bends over to pick it up. The camera tilts up with him as he stands up straight again. He comes forward and goes off.*

46. LS: *he approaches, stops again (*MS*), and looks down; this time he picks up a piece of rope, and stares in front of him.*

47. LS *of something lying in the leaves.*

48. *A closer shot of the object: it is an amulet case.*

49. CU *of the woodcutter, who then moves to the right into* MS *range (pan) but stumbles; he jumps back with a look of horror on his face.*

50. MS: *the stiffly raised hands of a corpse are in front of him. A gong is sounded.*

51. CU *of the woodcutter's face; he leaps back, turns around and, his back to the camera, runs into the woods, dropping his ax as he goes.*

52. MS: *the camera moves rapidly alongside the woodcutter as he runs panic-stricken through the woods. His speech runs over this and the next two shots.*

    WOODCUTTER (*off-screen*): I ran as fast as I could to tell the police. That was three days ago. Then the police called me to testify.

53. MS: *the camera continues to move with the woodcutter.*

54. MS: *the camera continues with him. (Wipe.)*

55. MS *of the woodcutter kneeling on the sand of the prison courtyard.*

> WOODCUTTER: Yes, sir. It was I who found the body first. (*Pause. He is obviously being questioned though we hear only his answers.*) Was there a sword or anything? No, sir. Nothing at all. Only a woman's hat, caught on a branch . . . and a man's hat that had been trampled on. And a piece of rope . . . and further off an amulet case of red brocade. (*Pause.*) Yes, sir. Yes, that was all I saw. I swear it. (*He bows.*) (*Wipe.*)

56. MS *of the priest kneeling in the prison courtyard. Behind him is the woodcutter. The priest is testifying.*

> PRIEST: Yes, sir, I saw the murdered man when he was still alive. Well, it was about three days ago. It was in the afternoon. Yes, it was on the road between Sekiyama and Yamashina.

57. *The priest is walking along a road which winds through a bamboo grove. Music in. Pan as he approaches the camera and passes it. He stops, back to camera. From the opposite direction a samurai approaches, leading a horse by the bridle. On the horse is a woman, sitting sidesaddle. The priest steps back and looks after them (pan); they recede into the distance.*

> PRIEST (*off-screen*): Her hat had a veil. I couldn't see her face. The man was armed. He had a sword, bow and arrows. (*A gong sounds.*)

58. MS *of the priest in the prison courtyard, as in 56.*

> PRIEST: I never thought I would see him again; then, to see him dead like that. Oh, it is true—life is ephemeral, as fleeting as the morning dew. But the pity of it. What a pity that he should have died like that. (*He bows.*) (*Wipe.*)

59. MS: *the police agent is proudly testifying. Beside him, tied up, sits the bandit, Tajomaru. Behind them sit the woodcutter and the priest.*

POLICE AGENT: Yes, it was I who caught Tajomaru. Yes, indeed. That very same notorious bandit who has been so much talked about, even in the outskirts of the city.

60. CU *of the bandit gazing vacantly up at the sky, the voice of the agent continuing.*

61. *The sky, filled with huge summer clouds.*

POLICE AGENT (*continuing, off-screen*): Yes, this is the very same bandit, Tajomaru, your honor. When I finally caught him . . .

62. MS *of the agent testifying, as in 59.*

POLICE AGENT: . . . he was dressed like he is now, and carried that Korean sword. It was toward evening, day before yesterday, by the riverbank at Katsura. (*Dolly to* CU *of agent. Music in, continuing into next shot.*)

63. *The riverbank. Camera pans to follow as agent walks along the bank. He hears a horse neigh, and runs along the bank (away from camera) toward a man seen in* LS *range lying as though in agony. He leans over to lift the man and loses his grip, stumbling back into the river.*

64. MS: *Tajomaru, in the foreground, groaning, apparently in agony, writhing in the sand. In the background, the agent in the river. The camera travels left from them to reveal, farther down along the bank, a bow, arrows, and finally a horse.*

POLICE AGENT (*off-screen*): There was a black-lacquered quiver holding seventeen arrows in all—they all had hawk feathers. The bow was bound in leather . . . and there was a gray horse.

65. MS *of the agent in the prison courtyard; the camera backs away from* CU *of him to same position as shot 59.*

POLICE AGENT: And they all belonged to the murdered man. But just
   imagine a fierce bandit like Tajomaru here being thrown by the very
   animal that he himself had stolen. It was retribution.

*The bandit wheels toward him threateningly, hisses through his teeth,
then bursts into laughter.*

TAJOMARU: Retribution? Don't be stupid. On that day . . .

66. LS: *a hill, low clouds. Triumphant music. Tajomaru, shouting, gallops
   across and off the screen in low foreground.*

TAJOMARU (*continuing, off-screen*): . . . while I was riding that gray
   horse I suddenly got very thirsty.[2]

2. In some prints, this voice-over is cut and Tajomaru seems to begin this speech in shot 67.

67. MS *of Tajomaru, continuing in the prison courtyard.*

TAJOMARU: So when I got near Osaka Pass I had a drink at a stream.

68. LS *from above. Tajomaru, stretched on the ground, drinks from a small stream. His heavy panting is heard.*

69. MS *of Tajomaru in the prison courtyard, as in 67.*

TAJOMARU: There must have been a snake or something in the upper stream, because after a few hours I began to have this terrible colic. Toward evening it got so I couldn't bear it any longer and so I got off the horse and lay down. (*Dolly back to the two-shot [59] of Tajomaru and the police agent.*) And you thought I'd fallen off—hah! (*He hisses and kicks the quiver lying in front of the agent.*) It takes a pretty stupid person to have an idea that stupid.

70. MCU *of Tajomaru.*

TAJOMARU: No, I'm telling the truth. I know you're going to cut off my head sooner or later—I'm not hiding anything. It was me, Tajomaru, who killed that man. Yes, I did it. It was a hot afternoon, about three days ago, that I first saw them. And then all of a sudden there was this cool breeze. If it hadn't been for that breeze, maybe I wouldn't have killed him.

The bell-like music, like distant wind chimes, is heard as he concludes; the music continues into the next shot.

71. *In the woods; the camera tilts from the great crown of an enormous tree down to its roots to reveal the bandit sprawled out sleeping at the base of another huge tree nearby. Music denoting the traveling couple fades in over the tinkling bells.*

72. MS *of Tajomaru asleep; the camera dollies in to closer range and pans around to reveal the samurai leading the horse on which the woman is riding.*

73. *Camera travels backward as it shows the pair coming down the road.*

74. MCU *of the bandit; he looks sleepily in their direction.*

75. MS *of the woman on horseback, her face barely visible through the veil of her hat.*

76. MCU, *as in 74: Tajomaru closes his eyes, scratches, appears to be falling asleep again, but then glances again in the direction of the couple.*

77. LS: *the pair approach the "sleeping" figure.*

78. MS: *profile of the samurai as he sees Tajomaru and hesitates.*

79. MCU, *as in 74: Tajomaru, his eyes half-open, staring back at the samurai.*

80. MS: *the samurai, now seen from in front, continues to assess Tajomaru.*

81. MCU, *as in 74: Tajomaru staring back; he scratches his leg lazily, closing his eyes again.*

82. MCU: *the samurai decides to move on, leading the horse toward the camera.*

83. MCU *of Tajomaru, as in 74, his eyes shut. Then, to the sound of the bell-like music, a fresh breeze stirs his hair; he opens his eyes, looks in the couple's direction, and gives a start.*

84. CU *of the feet of the woman, gently swinging with the movements of the horse; the camera tilts up to show her face as the veil is blown aside.*

85. ECU *of Tajomaru, now wide-awake, looking.*

86. CU *of the woman on horseback (pan), her veil parting to reveal her face fully.*

87. ECU, *as in 85: Tajomaru begins to raise himself up.*

88. MS *from behind Tajomaru, now in a sitting position. Pan as the horse and couple move past him in the background. Tajomaru turns and looks after them, then sinks back under the tree as they continue to move farther down the road.*

89. MS *of Tajomaru, from in front. His sword rests between his legs, and now he slowly pulls it closer to him.*

90. *In the prison courtyard, Tajomaru continues his testimony, as in 70.*

TAJOMARU: It was just a glimpse. First I saw her, then she was gone—I thought I had seen an angel. And right then I decided I would take her, that I'd have her even if I had to kill the man. . . . (*He laughs.*) But if I could do it without killing him, then that would be all the better. So I decided not to kill him but to somehow get the woman alone. The road to Yamashina was hardly the place to do it though.

91. LS: *Tajomaru runs through the woods toward the camera. Chase music in.*

92. LS *from the side; the camera travels with him as he races along.*

93. MS: *he runs down a slope (pan).*

94. MS: *pan to follow him as he leaps over a small brook and approaches the couple in the background. Music out.*

95. MS *of Tajomaru's back, the couple visible over his shoulder. The samurai stops and turns.*

    SAMURAI: What do you want?

96. MCU *of Tajomaru. He stares back at the samurai, absently slaps at a mosquito that has landed on his neck, then walks (pan) behind the horse (MS), glancing up at the woman.*

97. MCU *as Tajomaru eyes the pair, then walks to the front of the horse (MS) and crouches down.*

    SAMURAI (*off-screen*): What is it?

98. MS *from behind the samurai as he approaches Tajomaru.*

    SAMURAI (*threateningly*): What do you want?

    Tajomaru rises and crosses back behind the horse (pan), into a clearing. As the samurai crosses in front of the horse into the clearing, Tajomaru suddenly draws his sword and swings it smartly—the samurai at once reaches for his own sword, but the bandit laughs loudly, for he is merely displaying his.

    TAJOMARU: Isn't that splendid? Just look!

99. MS: *reverse angle from behind Tajomaru as, in profile, he proudly raises his sword.*

100. MS *of Tajomaru as he steps up to the samurai and presents the sword, hilt first.*

> TAJOMARU: Here, take it. Look at it. (*The samurai makes no move to accept it.*) Near here I found this old tomb (*points past camera*) with lots of things like this in it. I broke it open and inside found swords, daggers, mirrors. . . . I buried them all here in the woods and no one but me knows where. But if you're interested I might sell some of them to you cheap. (*Presents the sword again.*)

101. MCU *from reverse angle as Tajomaru holds out the sword. The samurai abruptly takes it and examines it. Tajomaru glances in the woman's direction and scratches his cheek. (Wipe.)*

102. *The forest, enormous trees. Idyllic music. The camera tilts down to reveal the woman sitting on the ground alone, the horse grazing behind her.*

103. CU *of the bow and arrows, which have been left lying on the ground near the woman.*

104. LS: *moving generally to the left, the bandit and the samurai are climbing a slope in the woods; a traveling shot from above and behind them. Music with drums accompanies the trek through the woods.*

105. MS *from above and in front of them as they continue up the slope (pan), now to the right, then turning.*

106. LS: *they push on to the left through the woods (pan).*

107. MS: *pan as they go on. Suddenly Tajomaru stops and draws his sword. The man recoils, thinking the bandit is about to fight. Tajomaru laughs and with a shout pokes his sword toward the samurai. Then he begins slashing at the obstructing underbrush with the sword (pan).*

108. CU: *pan as the bandit hacks his way forward. He pauses.*

> TAJOMARU: It's over there in that grove.

109. CU *of the samurai, eyeing the bandit.*

SAMURAI: You walk ahead of me.

110. MS: *samurai in the foreground; Tajomaru, in the background, waits, then turns from the camera and starts out, leading the way for the samurai.*

111. MS: *Tajomaru, hacking through the underbrush, leads the way as the two come toward the camera, which tracks backward.*

112. MS: *now the camera tracks forward and follows their backs.*

113. MS: *they approach the camera; it pans as they go off to the left. They proceed into the brush, away from camera.*

114. MS: *they approach from LS. Tajomaru stops and gestures.*

TAJOMARU: It's over there. (*He replaces his sword in its scabbard.*)

The samurai moves past and in front of him (pan), and stands looking with his back to Tajomaru, who now is out of frame.

115. MS *of Tajomaru—pan as he moves toward, then past the camera and attacks the other man, knocking him to the ground. Fight music punctuates the action. They roll over each other, but Tajomaru kicks the samurai away, then leaps through the air after him. The remainder of the fight is never seen, for as Tajomaru lands atop the samurai, a wipe leads into shot 116.*

116. MS: *a traveling shot of Tajomaru running to the right through the woods. He pauses for a moment to point back in the direction of the samurai, laughing and shouting.*

117. CU: *the camera continues to travel with him.*

118. LS: *still running and laughing loudly, he starts down a hill.*

119. LS *from the bottom of the hill. Tajomaru descends, stops, and peers through the bushes* MCU.

120. *Seen from over his shoulder, far below, stands the woman, waiting by a small brook. She crouches to dangle her hand in the water.*

121. MS: *a closer view of the waiting woman.*

122. MCU, *as in 119: Tajomaru looks down at her, his eyes wide.*

123. MCU *of the woman, serenely passing the time.*

124. MCU, *as in 119: Tajomaru peering down.*

125. CU *of the woman's hand, playing with the water as it flows gently past. Suddenly her hand stops.*

126. MCU *of the woman from the side as she turns abruptly to the camera, puzzled, and lifts her veil.*

127. MCU, *as in 119: Tajomaru sees she has noticed something and leaps forward from his hiding place.*

128. MS *from reverse angle. Tajomaru's back is to the camera as he bounds down toward her away from the camera.*

129. *Reverse angle from over the woman's shoulder in the foreground. Tajomaru runs swiftly up to her and stops, panting, in front of her.*

TAJOMARU: Something terrible has happened. Your husband has been bitten by a snake.

130. MS: *reverse angle of the woman from behind Tajomaru. Shocked, she stands up, removing her hat.*

131. MCU *of the bareheaded woman; she stares incredulously at the bandit.*

132. MCU *of Tajomaru in the prison courtyard, continuing his testimony.*

>   TAJOMARU: She became very pale and stared at me as though her eyes were frozen. She looked like a child when it turns suddenly serious. The sight of her made me jealous of that man; I started to hate him. I wanted to show her what he looked like, all tied up like that. I hadn't even thought of a thing like that before, but now I did.

133. MS: *a traveling shot of Tajomaru running to the left through the woods, pulling the woman after him. Travel music begins.*

134. MS *of the woman; a traveling shot as she is pulled along by the wrist.*

135. CU: *a traveling shot of her hat dragging behind her; it snags on a branch (camera stops) and is left behind.*

136. *They run from* LS *up to the camera, which pans to reveal the samurai, tightly bound up, sitting in the clearing where Tajomaru attacked him. The woman stops abruptly.*

137. MS *of the samurai, helpless.*

138. MCU *of the woman who stands transfixed by the sight of her husband, Tajomaru behind her. The bandit steps forward past her.*

139. LS *from behind the husband, the woman and Tajomaru in the background: Tajomaru steps back to look at both of them.*

140. MS *from behind the husband, the woman in the background.*

141. MS *from behind the bandit, the husband in the background.*

142. MS *from the side of the woman, the bandit in the background.*

143. MS *from the side of the bandit, the woman in the background.*

144. MS *from behind the husband, the bandit in the background. The samurai looks toward his wife.*

145. MS *from the side of the woman, her husband in the background. The camera moves swiftly toward her and pans around then away from her* (MS). CU: *she suddenly turns to attack the bandit with her dagger. She races toward him, her weapon outstretched, but he dodges the thrust and springs around to look at her with admiring disbelief.*

146. CU *of her frenzied face as she regains her balance and whirls to charge again.*

147. MS *from behind her as she runs at him again (pan); he dodges, she turns and charges at him with the dagger held straight before her. Hysterical now, she misses and stumbles out of sight. The camera remains on Tajomaru's laughing face.*

148. MS: *Tajomaru in the foreground, the woman in the background; she dives forward and grabs his leg, but he pulls free.*

149. MCU *of Tajomaru; he stares down at her, excited by her desperate spirit.*

150. MCU *of the woman, stretched on the ground; she menaces him with the dagger held straight up at him, every muscle tense and ready.*

TAJOMARU (*off-screen*): She was fierce . . .

151. MCU *of Tajomaru, as in 149; his admiration is unbounded.*

TAJOMARU: . . . determined.

152. MCU *of the woman, as in 150; she won't relent.*

153. MS *of the two of them; he continues to stand over her, silent, watchful.*

TAJOMARU (*off-screen*): She fought like a cat.[3]

She starts to crawl away, then rises, slashes at him.

---

3. This line is not heard in some U.S. release prints.

154. MS *from reverse angle as he grabs her.*

155. MCU: *Tajomaru behind the woman. He shouts in pain as she sinks her teeth into his forearm; he flings her away and (pan) she trips to the ground.*

156. MCU *of Tajomaru; he licks his wound and moves forward.*

157. MCU *of the woman as she rises to attack again.*

158. LS: *she chases him to the right, wildly slicing the air with her dagger (pan). He circles a tree and continues in the opposite direction (pan).*

159. MS: *he reaches another tree, swings around it, and waits for her next move. She thrusts at him, sobbing, and they chase each other around the tree.*

160. MS *from right. He runs off (traveling shot); she follows, but collapses, exhausted; he stands jubilant over her.*

161. LS: *the woman in the foreground, in close range, helplessly sobbing; Tajomaru in the background. He stalks up to her, she lunges yet again, but now he grabs and holds her.*

162. MCU *of the husband watching them; he bows his head.*

163. CU: *the woman claws Tajomaru's face; he wrests his head free and pushes her to the ground (camera tilts down). She struggles but he kisses her.*

164. *The sky seen through the branches of the trees (pan).*

165. CU *of the bandit kissing her; she stares straight up.*

166. *The sky seen through the overhead branches (pan), as in 164.*

167. CU *from reverse angle; Tajomaru holding her, kissing her.*

168. *The sky and trees, as in 164. The camera has stopped panning; now the sun is seen shining brilliantly through the branches. Bell-like music begins.*

169. ECU *from reverse angle; Tajomaru kissing the woman, as she stares blankly up at the sun.*

170. *The sun through the branches, as in 168; slowly the scene goes out of focus.*

171. ECU, *as in 169. The woman closes her eyes.*

172. CU *of the dagger in her hand, Tajomaru tightly gripping her wrist. Her fingers loosen, the dagger drops to the ground.*

173. CU *of the dagger sticking point first in the ground.*

174. MS *of Tajomaru's back, the woman in his arms. The camera slowly dollies toward them during the kiss. Her hand encircles his back, her fingers move caressingly; she tightens her grip on him. Shot ends with ECU of the back of Tajomaru's head and an area of the woman's face as the kiss continues.*

175. MS: *in the prison courtyard, Tajomaru is laughing and kicking his feet exultantly.*

> TAJOMARU: And so I had her—just as I'd planned, and without killing the husband. And that was how I did it. Besides, I hadn't intended to kill him. But then . . .

176. *Shot of Tajomaru's back, beginning in close range, as he walks away from the camera to go off into the woods; the woman rushes after him (LS).*

177. MS *from reverse angle. She throws herself at his feet.*

> WOMAN: Wait. Stop. One of you must die. Either you or my husband.

178. MCU *of her husband. Bound up, he stares without expression.*

179. MCU *of Tajomaru staring at the samurai; then he looks down at the woman.*

180. MCU *of the woman kneeling, seen from over Tajomaru's shoulder.*

> WOMAN: Either you or he must die. To be doubly disgraced, disgraced before two men, is more than I can bear.

181. MCU *of Tajomaru looking down at her.*

182. MCU, *as in 180: the woman continues to speak intensely.*

> WOMAN: I want . . . I will belong to whoever kills the other.

183. CU *of the woman; her honor at stake, she looks up expectantly at the bandit.*

184. ECU *of Tajomaru. A fierce resolution comes over his face.*

185. MCU *of the woman on the ground. Tajomaru walks away to the samurai in the background* (LS). *The woman remains in the foreground with lowered eyes. Tajomaru takes out his sword.*

186. MS: *Tajomaru cuts the ropes binding the samurai, and holds out the unsheathed sword he has robbed from him. The samurai whips the sword from its scabbard and slashes at Tajomaru. The samurai then springs to his feet and they begin to fight (pan). They move away from the camera into the background.*

187. MS: *the two duel, slashing and parrying. Martial music.*

188. MCU: *Tajomaru turns, thrusts at the samurai.*

189. MCU *of Tajomaru's sword as the samurai dodges; Tajomaru pulls back and they cross swords again.*

190. MS: *the two of them fighting, Tajomaru in the foreground; the bandit heads away from the camera and scrambles up a slight incline.*

191. MS: *he slips and falls, but remains there in a sitting position, glaring defiantly at his opponent.*

192. MS *from reverse angle. The bandit's back in the foreground, the samurai visible below. Tajomaru scratches idly, then charges down the incline past the other man. Now in the background, the bandit turns and starts to walk insouciantly away, then whirls on his opponent.*

193. *Tajomaru lunges forward, the samurai backs out of the frame, Tajomaru follows. The samurai charges back into the frame, followed again by the bandit. They fight toward the background; the samurai stumbles.*

194. CU: *the samurai, stumbling, falls to a sitting position.*

195. MS: *Tajomaru, in the background, circles menacingly around the samurai in the foreground.*

196. MCU, *as in 194, of the samurai on guard, ready to ward off Tajomaru's attack.*

197. MCU *of the bandit jabbing at the fallen samurai.*

198. MCU, *as in 194, of the samurai warding off the thrust.*

199. MS, *as in 197, of the bandit circling (pan), brandishing his sword, sometimes feinting a lunge.*

200. *The samurai, as in 194, still in a sitting position, turns with Tajomaru.*

201. MCU, *as in 197, of the bandit circling (pan) in the other direction.*

202. MCU, *as in 194, of the samurai, still sitting, sword in a defensive position.*

203. MS, *as in 197, of the bandit (pan) taunting, feinting—finally he lunges.*

204. ECU: *the samurai, who has kept in his free hand the rope that had bound him, now whips the rope at Tajomaru.*

205. CU, *as in 197: the bandit wards off the rope.*

206. MS: *the samurai is on his feet again, and the two cross swords, circling around so that the samurai's back is to the camera.*

207. MS *from reverse angle. The two men fight, running, struggling; they begin to duel around a tree, Tajomaru pursuing.*

208. *Camera dollies in to a closer shot of the two men fighting around the tree.*

209. LS *through the bushes of a thicket. The samurai is forced back into the thicket, his back to the camera; then he stumbles and falls on his back. Tajomaru moves in on him. The samurai's sword has become entangled in the undergrowth. Dolly in to MS of Tajomaru, who laughs, raises his sword to throw it, and spears the samurai with a mighty heave. Tajomaru stands looking down.*

210. MS: *in the prison courtyard, Tajomaru continues.*

TAJOMARU: I wanted to kill him honestly, since I had to kill him. And he
fought really well. We crossed swords over twenty-three times. Think of
that! No one had ever crossed over twenty with me before. Then I killed
him. (*He laughs.*)

*The camera has dollied back to reveal the police agent, as well as the
priest and the woodcutter in the background.*

TAJOMARU (*answering the unheard voice of the official questioner*):
What's that? The woman? Oh, she wasn't around anywhere. Probably
got frightened and ran away. She must have been really upset. Anyway,
when I came down the path again I found the horse grazing there.
About that woman—it was her temper that interested me, but she
turned out to be just like any other woman. I didn't even look for her.
(*Pause.*) What? His sword? Oh, I sold that in town on the same day,
then drank the money up. (*Pause.*) Her dagger? I remember, it looked

valuable, had some kind of inlay in it. You know what I did? I forgot all about it. What a fool thing to do. Walked off and forgot it. That was the biggest mistake I ever made. (*Laughs uproariously, kicking his feet on the ground.*)

211. MS *of the rain pouring off the eaves of the Rashomon gate; the sound of the great downpour. Tilt down to reveal the three men below.*

212. MS *of the woodcutter, in the foreground, and the commoner, sitting by a fire; the commoner stretches and yawns.*

COMMONER: Oh, that Tajomaru, he's famous for that sort of thing. He's worse than all the other bandits in Kyoto. Why, last fall a young girl went off with her maid to worship at the Toribe Temple and they found them murdered there afterwards. He must have done it. (*He rises to fetch some wood.*)

213. LS: *the priest in the foreground; the commoner, in the background, continues talking as he crosses behind the priest.*

COMMONER: They say the woman ran away and left her horse behind. I just bet he killed her.

He pulls some loose planks from the side of the gate. The priest rises to walk back to the commoner.

PRIEST: But the woman turned up in prison too, you know.

The commoner turns to listen.

214. MS *from reverse angle, commoner in the foreground. The priest approaches the commoner.*

PRIEST: It seems she went to seek refuge at some temple and the police found her there.

The voice of the woodcutter cuts across this.

WOODCUTTER *(off-screen):* It's a lie!

215. MCU *of the woodcutter, the priest and commoner visible in the background.*

   WOODCUTTER: It's a lie. They're all lies! Tajomaru's confession, the woman's story—they're lies!

   COMMONER: Well, men are only men. That's why they lie. (*He pulls a board loose and turns to speak again.*) They can't tell the truth, not even to themselves.

   PRIEST: That may be true. But it's because men are so weak. That's why they lie. That's why they must deceive themselves.

   COMMONER: Not another sermon! (*He starts to move forward.*)

216. MS *of the commoner, leaning forward as he puts the wood on the fire.*

   COMMONER: I don't mind a lie. Not if it's interesting. What kind of story did she tell? (*He looks up.*)

217. MS *of the priest.*

   PRIEST: Hers was a completely different story from the bandit's. (*He comes up and kneels between the others, the camera panning with him.*) Everything was different.

218. CU *of the priest.*

   PRIEST: Tajomaru talked about her temper, her strength. I saw nothing like that at all. I found her very pitiful. I felt great compassion for her.

219. LS *of the prison courtyard, the woman prostrate in the foreground, the woodcutter and priest kneeling in the background. The main thematic music begins softly and continues, almost uninterrupted, throughout the woman's version of the story. At times gentle, at other times frenzied, it is the only musical theme through shot 254. The woman is bent over weeping; she raises her head.*

220. MS *of the woman, who slowly raises the upper half of her body.*

   WOMAN: And then, after having taken advantage of me, he told me—oh, so proudly—that he was the famous bandit Tajomaru. And then he sneered at my husband.

221. MCU *as she continues, now more possessed.*

   WOMAN: Oh, how terrible it must have been for him. But the more he struggled, the tighter the ropes became. I couldn't stand it. Not even realizing what I was doing, I ran toward him, or tried to.

222. LS: *the woods. With her back to the camera, the woman runs toward her husband; the bandit pushes past her, knocking her down, and goes up to the husband bound by the tree. He takes the husband's sword and starts to leave.*

223. MS *of Tajomaru as he turns to sneer at the husband. The woman's sobs are heard and Tajomaru begins to laugh and point at the husband, then turns away.*

224. LS *as Tajomaru stops to laugh again, jumping up and down; then he runs away from the camera, disappearing into the woods.*

225. LS: *the woman lies weeping on the ground by her husband.*

226. LS: *the same, from nearer.*

227. MS: *the same, nearer still.*

228. MCU *of the woman, sobbing; finally she raises her head to look brokenheartedly at her husband.*

229. MCU *of her husband, in profile. He stares at the ground.*

230. MCU, *as in 228: she looks at him, then begins to rise.*

231. LS *from behind the woman as she rises and rushes toward her husband in the background and throws herself on him.*

232. CU *from over his shoulder. She sobs on his breast, looks up, and is shocked by what she sees.*

233. CU *of the husband from over her shoulder. He looks at her coldly, cynically.*

234. MCU *of the woman in the prison courtyard as she continues: the wood-cutter and priest visible in the background.*

WOMAN: Even now I remember his eyes. . . . What I saw in them was not sorrow, not even anger. It was . . . a cold hatred of me.

235. MS *in the woods, the woman seen over her husband's shoulder. She pulls herself away from him, staring at him. As she speaks, she moves from side to side before him, the camera moving with her.*

WOMAN: Don't look at me like that. Don't! Beat me, kill me if you must, but don't look at me like that. Please don't!

236. CU: *she covers her face with her hands and starts to sink back to the ground.*

237. ECU *of the top of her head as she lies shaking and sobbing.*

238. CU: *suddenly she looks up, glances around, starts to rise.*

239. LS: *the pair in the background; in the foreground is the dagger, still stick-*

ing point first in the ground. She rises to her feet, comes forward and retrieves it, and rushes back to her husband, starting to cut his bonds.

240. CU: *the dagger cutting through the rope.*

241. MS *over the husband's shoulder; she extends the dagger to him.*

WOMAN: Then kill me if you will. Kill me with one stroke—quickly!

The camera dollies toward her face, then pans around to show the husband still staring at her as before.

242. MCU: *she looks up imploringly, rises, and starts to back away.*

243. MS: *the camera dollies with her as she backs away.*

WOMAN: Oh, don't! Please don't!

She raises her hands to her face, still clutching the dagger.

244. CU *of the husband's hard, unmoved face.*

WOMAN (*off-screen*): Don't—don't look at me like that!

245. MCU: *she comes forward again, dagger extended.*

WOMAN: Don't.

246. CU, *as in 244, of the husband staring; her sobs are heard.*

247. MS, *as in 245, of the woman, backing off again, crying.*

248. CU, *as in 244, of the husband.*

249. MS, *as in 245. The woman continues to move, the camera seeming to weave with her painful approach and retreat before her husband. She holds the dagger almost absent-mindedly; her desperation grows.*

250. CU, *as in 244, of the husband, staring implacably.*

251. MCU *of the woman as she moves steadily forward now; her world forever destroyed, she holds the dagger high, without seeming to be aware of it. The camera tracks with her in the direction of her husband until she suddenly lunges off screen.*

252. MS, *as in 234, of the woman in the prison courtyard, continuing her testimony.*

> WOMAN: And then I fainted. When I opened my eyes and looked around, I saw there, in my husband's chest, the dagger. (*She begins to weep again.*) I didn't know what to do. I ran through the forest—I must have, although I don't remember. Then I found myself standing by a pond . . .

253. *Shot of a lake, illuminated by a low sun, a strong breeze moving over the surface.*

> WOMAN (*continuing, off-screen*): . . . at the foot of a hill.

254. MS, *as in 234, of the woman in the prison courtyard.*

> WOMAN: I threw myself into it. I tried to kill myself. But, I failed. (*She sobs.*) What could a poor helpless woman like me do? (*She sinks to the ground.*)

255. *The steps of the Rashomon gate with the rain pouring down. The dreary, loud sound of the rain. Visible above the steps are the three men, seated. The camera tilts up as the commoner stands; he comes forward, looks out at the sky, spits disgustedly, and turns back to the group.*

256. MS: *he rejoins the other two around the fire (pan).*

> COMMONER: I see. But the more I listen the more mixed up I get. (*He sits down.*) Women lead you on with their tears; they even fool themselves. Now if I believed what she said I'd really be mixed up.

PRIEST: But according to the husband's story . . .

COMMONER: But he's dead. How could a dead man talk?

PRIEST: He spoke through a medium.

WOODCUTTER: Lies. (*He rises and comes toward the camera.*) His story was all lies.

PRIEST: Dead men tell no lies.

257. MCU *of the commoner, in the foreground, and the priest.*

COMMONER: All right, priest—why is that?

PRIEST: They must not. I must not believe that men are so sinful.

258. MCU *of the two from reverse angle.*

COMMONER: Oh, I don't object to that. After all, who's honest nowadays? Look, everyone wants to forget unpleasant things, so they make up stories. It's easier that way. (*Grinning, he bites into a piece of fruit. The priest looks distraught.*) But never mind. Let's hear this dead man's story.

259. *The ceiling and beams of the great gate illuminated by a tremendous flash of lightning.*

260. LS *from above the three men as they look up. A roll of thunder is heard.*

261. MS *of a fallen statue outside the gate. The rain falls even harder, flooding in rapid cascades past the statue.*

262. CU *of the statue.*

263. CU *of a hand bell being violently shaken in the air. The scene has abruptly shifted back to the prison courtyard.*

264. MS *of the medium, a woman, her hair and robes blowing in the wind. She is rattling the bell, dancing madly. The bell clatters, the wind howls, and a weird, unearthly voice drones on like a record player slowing down. A drum beats slowly. The wind, voice, and drum continue through shot 273.*

265. LS *from above the medium. Behind her kneel the woodcutter and the priest. She circles the altar which has been placed in the courtyard, shaking the bell.*

266. CU, *as in 263, of the bell being shaken.*

267. MLS *of the medium writhing about on her feet. She begins to turn dizzily in circles. Suddenly she stops completely still.*

268. MCU *of the medium, now possessed by the other world.*

269. CU *of the bell dropping from her hand.*

270. MCU, *as in 268: she turns abruptly in the direction of the camera.*

271. LS: *she rushes toward the foreground and stands, mouth open, her eyes wild, as the camera dollies in. Her mouth begins to move and suddenly the voice of the dead man is heard.*

> SAMURAI-MEDIUM (*as though at a great distance*): I am in darkness now. I am suffering in the darkness. Cursed be those who cast me into this hell of darkness. (*The medium starts to fall.*)

272. MS *of the medium falling behind the altar to the ground. She moves convulsively on the ground, the camera panning with her.*

273. MS: *she sits upright as the camera dollies in. Her mouth opens and over the sound of the wind the voice of the samurai is heard.*

> SAMURAI-MEDIUM: The bandit, after attacking my wife, sat down beside her and tried to console her.

(The sound of the unearthly voice and drum stops abruptly.)

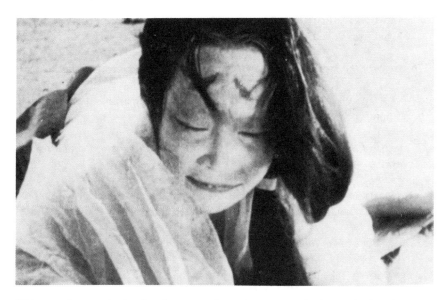

274. LS: *the woods. In the clearing where the rape took place, the bandit is sitting beside the woman, talking to her, touching her arm to get her attention. The samurai's story is accompanied by a somber musical theme which plays over most of the scenes through shot 305.*

SAMURAI-MEDIUM (*off-screen*): She sat there on the leaves, looking down, looking at nothing. The bandit was cunning.

Camera dollies back to reveal the husband bound in the foreground.

SAMURAI-MEDIUM (*off-screen*): He told her that after she had given herself, she would no longer be able to live with her husband—why didn't she go with him, the bandit, rather than remain behind to be unhappy with her husband? He said he had only attacked her because of his great love for her.

The husband turns his head toward them.

275. CU *of the wife as she looks up as though she believes what Tajomaru is saying, her eyes dreamy.*

SAMURAI-MEDIUM (*off-screen*): My wife looked at him, her face soft, her eyes veiled.

276. MCU *of the medium in the prison courtyard, as at the end of shot 273.*

SAMURAI-MEDIUM: Never, in all of our life together, had I seen her more beautiful.

277. MCU *of the husband in the woods; he stares at the others, then closes his eyes.*

SAMURAI-MEDIUM (*off-screen*): And what did my beautiful wife reply to the bandit in front of her helpless husband?

278. MS: *the woman looks up at Tajomaru, imploringly.*

WOMAN: Take me. Take me away with you.

279. *The prison courtyard. A blank sky; the medium's face rises into view, the wind whipping her hair. From* MCU *range she runs away from the camera, which pursues her; she then moves forward, the camera retreating before her. Through all this, the unearthly voice fades in and out.*

SAMURAI-MEDIUM: That is what she said. (*The medium turns away, then abruptly faces the camera again.*) But that is not all she did, or else I would not now be in darkness.

280. MS: *in the woods, from behind the husband's back. Tajomaru picks up the husband's sword and moves off-screen. He returns, leading the woman off into the woods.*

281. MCU *of Tajomaru as he is jerked to a stop by the woman.*

282. MS *of the woman holding Tajomaru by the hand. She points toward her husband.*

WOMAN: Kill him. As long as he is alive I cannot go with you. (*She moves behind Tajomaru, clutching him.*) Kill him!

283. MS *of the medium in the prison courtyard, the wind howling about her.*

> SAMURAI-MEDIUM: I still hear those words. (*The medium writhes in circles on her knees.*) They are like a wind blowing me to the bottom of this dark pit. Has anyone ever uttered more pitiless words? Even the bandit was shocked to hear them.

284. ECU *of the woman in the woods, clinging to the bandit's shoulder, digging her nails into him.*

> WOMAN: Kill him!

285. LS: *the bandit and the woman from behind the husband's back; the woman takes a step toward the husband, pointing at him.*

> WOMAN: Kill him—kill him!

286. MCU *of Tajomaru, yanking the woman back to him. The look in his eyes makes her back off.*

287. LS, *as in 285: the bandit throws the woman from him.*

288. MS *of the woman as she falls to the ground; the bandit places his foot on her back.*

289. CU *of the medium in the prison courtyard. She throws her head back and then forward and the dead man's laughter pours from her unmoving lips.*

290. LS: *Tajomaru, still standing over the woman, addresses the husband.*

> TAJOMARU: What do you want me to do with this woman? Kill her? Spare her? Just nod if you agree.

The camera dollies around to show the husband in profile.

> SAMURAI-MEDIUM (*off-screen*): For these words I almost forgave the bandit.

291. LS *of the husband in the background; in the foreground (*MS*) Tajomaru continues pressing the woman to the ground with his foot.*

> TAJOMARU: What do you want me to do? Kill her? Let her go?

Now Tajomaru walks toward the husband. As soon as he has gone a few steps, the woman springs up and runs away. Tajomaru turns to chase her, the camera panning to show them disappear among the trees. Her screams die away in the stillness of the woods.

292. LS *of the husband; still bound, he makes no effort to free himself.*

293. MS *of the husband.*

294. MCU *of the husband.*

295. *Dead leaves on the ground in the late afternoon sun.*

> SAMURAI-MEDIUM (*off-screen*): Hours later—I don't know how many.

296. MS *of the husband's back. Tajomaru appears in the background, on the far side of the clearing, stomping along, slashing in disgust with some rope at the bushes. He walks up to the husband and stands looking down.*

297. MS *from reverse angle. Tajomaru takes his sword and cuts the captive's bonds.*

TAJOMARU: Well, she got away. Now I'll have to worry about her talking. (*He turns and goes.*)

The husband looks off after him, then down, then up at the sky.

298. *Trees against the sky.*

SAMURAI-MEDIUM (*off-screen*): It was quiet.

299. *Dead leaves on the ground.*

SAMURAI-MEDIUM (*off-screen*): Then I heard someone crying . . .

The camera tilts up along the leaves to reveal the husband (MS). The bell-like tinkle of wind chimes is heard.

300. MCU *of the husband crying. The camera dollies back and he rises to his feet. He moves painfully (pan), rests his head against a tree. There is the soft sound of grief, but it comes from the husband himself.*

301. MCU *as he rests his head against the tree, sobbing. Finally he raises his head and begins to wander off, but stops when he notices something on the ground.*

302. MS *from behind the husband, the dagger sticking up before him. Slowly he goes to it, picks it up, and turns to walk back toward the camera, staring at the dagger.*

303. LS *as he moves forward into the clearing; he stops, raises the dagger high above his head and brutally thrusts it into his chest. He begins to fall.*

304. MS: *his falling motion is completed by the medium in the prison courtyard (priest and woodcutter sit in the background). The medium sinks down as though dead, then slowly sits up.*

305. MCU *of the medium.*

SAMURAI-MEDIUM: Everything was quiet—how quiet it was. It grew dark and a mist seemed to envelop me. I lay quietly in this stillness. Then someone seemed to approach me. Softly, gently. Who could it have been? Then someone's hand grasped the dagger and drew it out. (*The medium falls forward.*)

Music up and out.

306. LS: *in the shelter of the Rashomon gate, the priest and commoner are seated at the fire; the woodcutter is pacing up and down, the camera panning with him.*

307. MS *as the woodcutter stops in the background and turns to the others.*

WOODCUTTER: That's not true. There wasn't any dagger there—he was killed by a sword.

The commoner looks up from tending the fire. The woodcutter, very agitated, moves further into the background and sits down; the commoner rises and goes back to sit beside him.

308. *Reverse of preceding: in the foreground, the commoner sits next to the woodcutter; the priest is in the background.*

COMMONER: Now it's getting interesting. You must have seen the whole thing. Why didn't you tell the police?

WOODCUTTER: I didn't want to get involved.

COMMONER: But now you want to talk about it? Well, come on and tell us then. Yours seems the most interesting of all these stories.

309. *Reverse of the preceding: the priest in the foreground.*

PRIEST: I don't want to hear. I don't want to have to listen to any more horrible stories.

The commoner stands and comes forward to the priest.

COMMONER (*to the priest*): Stories like this are ordinary enough now. I
heard that demons used to live in the castle here by the gate, but they
all ran away, because what men do now horrified them so. (*He goes
back to the woodcutter.*)

310. CU *of the woodcutter and commoner.*

COMMONER: How much do you know about this story?

WOODCUTTER: I found a woman's hat . . .

COMMONER: You already said that.

WOODCUTTER: Then, when I'd walked about twenty yards farther, I heard a woman crying. I looked out from behind a bush and saw a man tied up. There was a woman crying. And there was Tajomaru.

COMMONER: Wait a minute. Then it was a lie when you said that you found the body?

WOODCUTTER: I didn't want to get involved.

COMMONER: All right, then. Go on. What was Tajomaru doing?

WOODCUTTER: He was down on his knees in front of the woman and seemed to be begging her to forgive him.

311. MS: *the woods. Tajomaru crouches by the woman, the samurai behind them. She is sobbing. From the beginning to the end of the woodcutter's story, there is a noticeable absence of music. The only sounds heard, aside from those made by the three people, are occasional noises natural to the woods.*

TAJOMARU: Until now, whenever I wanted to do anything bad, I always did it. It was for me and so it was good. But today is different. I've already taken you, but now I want you more and more—and I suffer. Go away with me. If you want, I'll marry you. Look. (*He bows his head low.*) I am Tajomaru, the famous bandit, known all over Miyako, and yet here I am on my knees in front of you.

312. MS *from the side. Tajomaru puts his hand on her, trying to soothe her.*

TAJOMARU: If you want, I'll even stop being a bandit. I've got enough money hidden away. You can live comfortably. And if you don't want me to steal, then I'll work hard—I'll even sell things in the street. I'll make you happy. I'll do anything to please you if you'll only come away with me, marry me. (*She only sobs the harder*).

313. MCU *from same angle as shot 311. Now the bandit tries to cajole her.*

TAJOMARU: Please say yes. If you don't, I'll have to kill you.

314. CU *of Tajomaru; he is becoming desperate.*

>   TAJOMARU: Don't cry. Answer. Tell me you'll be my wife. *(Unable to endure her silence, he suddenly pushes her).*

315. CU *from over Tajomaru's shoulder. He bends over solicitously again.*

>   TAJOMARU: Tell me.

316. MCU *from reverse angle. She sits up, almost in possession of herself.*

>   WOMAN: But, how could I answer? How could I, a woman, answer a question like that? (*She rises on her knees, the camera panning as she crawls over to the dagger and yanks it out of the ground.*)

317. MS *of the samurai, trussed up, in the foreground. Tajomaru, in the background, leaps aside and trips to the ground as the woman spins around with the dagger in her hand. But she is going to her husband with it. She cuts his bonds, then backs away sobbing, stumbling, and falls to the ground between the two men.*

318. MS *of Tajomaru, crouching at the ready.*

>   TAJOMARU: I understand. You mean that we men must decide. *(He reaches for his sword).*

319. LS *from behind Tajomaru. The samurai is struggling to free himself of the bonds now that the rope has been cut.*

320. MS *of the samurai as he jumps to his feet and nervously backs away.*

>   SAMURAI *(holding up his hand in front of him):* Stop! I refuse to risk my life for such a woman.

321. MCU: *Tajomaru looks at him hesitantly.*

322. MCU: *the woman sits up and looks in disbelief at her husband.*

323. MS: *the samurai, now haughty and self-possessed, walks up to his wife.*

SAMURAI: You shameless whore! Why don't you kill yourself?

324. LS *of the same, with Tajomaru in the foreground.*

SAMURAI (*to Tajomaru*): If you want her, I'll give her to you. I regret the loss of my horse much more than I will regret the loss of this woman. (*He turns away.*)

325. CU *of the woman; shocked, she turns from her husband to look at the bandit.*

326. MS: *she stares up at Tajomaru, who looks from her to the samurai.*

327. MLS: *the samurai in the foreground, Tajomaru staring at him. The samurai looks from one to the other.*

328. ECU: *Tajomaru looks at the woman distrustfully.*

329. CU: *she, sweating visibly, looks at Tajomaru.*

330. ECU, *as in 328: Tajomaru looks at her with distaste, wipes the sweat from his face.*

331. MS: *she watches him cross behind her as if to go, then gets up and runs after him (pan), both of them passing the husband, who stands immobile.*

WOMAN: Wait!

Tajomaru turns and calls back.

TAJOMARU: And don't try to follow me.

332. MS: *through Tajomaru's legs the woman is seen falling to the ground, her husband standing behind her. Then the husband steps forward.*

333. MCU *of the husband.*

SAMURAI: Don't waste your time in crying. No matter how hard you cry no one is going to be taken in by it.

334. MS *of Tajomaru as he steps forward to contradict.*

TAJOMARU: Don't talk like that to her. It's unmanly of you. After all, women cannot help crying. They are naturally weak.

335. MS *of the woman on the ground. Her weeping has been heard behind Tajomaru's words; now the sobs change and she laughs. She rises, screeching with hysterical laughter.*

WOMAN: It's not me, not me—it's you two who are weak. (*Pan as she goes to her husband.*) If you are my husband then why don't you kill this man? Then you can tell me to kill myself. That is what a real man would do. But you aren't a real man. That is why I was crying. I'm tired, tired of this farce. (*Pan as she crosses to the bandit.*) I thought that Tajomaru might find some way out. I thought that if he would only save me I would do anything for him.

336. CU *of the woman and Tajomaru. She spits in his face, then backs off, laughing (pan).*

WOMAN: But he's not a man either. He's just like my husband!

337. MS *of Tajomaru, looking shamefaced.*

WOMAN (*off-screen*): Just remember . . .

338. CU, *as in 335, of the woman.*

WOMAN: . . . that a woman loves only a real man. (*She moves nearer the bandit—pan.*) And when she loves, she loves madly, forgetting everything else. But a woman can be won only by strength—by the strength (*she is now at Tajomaru's side*) of the swords you are wearing.

339. MS *of the husband. He looks at her abjectly, then reaches for his sword.*

340. CU *of the husband as he moves toward Tajomaru now ready for a fight.*

341. MS *of all three; the woman and bandit, his sword already drawn, are in the foreground. From too far away, the samurai hurriedly swings his sword at Tajomaru, then backs quickly off. The woman smiles scornfully.*

342. MS: *the woman looks from one to the other, laughing and pointing gleefully.*

343. LS: *the two men, from high above, through the branches of the trees. They stand facing each other from a safe distance, the woman between them.*

344. MCU *of the woman. She seems to realize what is happening and a frightened look comes over her face. The sound of the combatants' nervous panting is heard now, and runs throughout the fight scene. It is a tense, gasping sound, unrelieved by music or any sound other than the occasional clash of swords.*

345. MS *of the bandit, circling, feinting, a concerned expression on his face.*

346. MS *of the samurai, advancing uncertainly.*

347. MS, *as in 345, of the bandit advancing.*

348. MS, *as in 346, of the samurai advancing.*

349. MCU *of the woman, watching fearfully. The camera dollies back until the two raised swords are visible in the frame. Suddenly the tips of the swords touch.*

350. LS: *the men recoil from the touching of the swords, stumbling backward away from each other. The samurai trips to the ground. Tajomaru runs after the samurai, but falls down himself. Both men swing wildly and blindly as they get to their feet and run in opposite directions from each other.*

351. LS: *Tajomaru in the foreground. The men are separated now by a great distance.*

352. CU *of the woman as she peeks out from behind the stump of a tree.*

353. MS *of the samurai, who has fallen against the side of a slope. Finally he stands up and advances.*

354. MS: *back-tracking shot of Tajomaru, advancing fearfully. His arm shaking violently, he seems almost unable to bear the weight of the sword. His breath comes in short gasps.*

355. MS, *as in 353, of the samurai advancing, terror written on his face.*

356. MS, *as in 354, of Tajomaru advancing.*

357. MS *of the woman, terrified; the camera dollies back as the men enter from either side of the frame. Each thrusts, frightening the other, but this time the samurai turns to run first at the sound of the woman's scream, and Tajomaru pursues him over to the slope (pan).*

358. MS: *they both slip and fall on the slope. Tajomaru thrusts at the samurai but misses, and his sword sticks in the ground. He can't extract it. Now the samurai swings, but the bandit rolls out of the way.*

359. LS: *Tajomaru continues to roll away (pan) to another part of the slope, which he tries to crawl up but fails to get a handhold.*

360. MS *as Tajomaru dodges another thrust.*

361. MS: *the samurai scampers after him but keeps stumbling and missing with his flailing swings.*

362. MS: *the bandit gets back to his sword but still can't pull it out. The samurai keeps lunging and missing; Tajomaru keeps dodging.*

363. LS: *the bandit runs and makes another attempt to mount the rise but falls*

*(pan). Now he runs away from the slope (pan) and falls by a tree stump.
The samurai aims another stroke wildly as Tajomaru falls behind the
stump.*

364. MS: *the samurai's sword lodges itself in the stump; Tajomaru seizes the
opportunity by leaping up at his assailant and pushing him down.*

365. MS: *Tajomaru tries to run past the fallen man but the samurai grabs him
by the ankle and pulls him down. Dragging the samurai after him, Tajomaru begins to inch toward his own sword.*

366. MS *from reverse angle. Slowly and with great effort, the bandit inches
toward his sword, the samurai holding onto his foot. Then Tajomaru kicks
him away and at last frees the sword from the ground.*

367. MS: *the samurai, still on the ground, backs off in alarm.*

368. MS: *Tajomaru, out of breath, rises shakily.*

369. LS: *pan as Tajomaru advances on the samurai, who pushes himself along
on his hands farther and farther into a thicket. Dolly in on the trapped
man, who screams.*

SAMURAI: I don't want to die! I don't want to die!

*Slight tilt upward to Tajomaru raising his sword and hurling it, out
of frame, into the man lying in front of him. Then he whirls around
triumphantly.*

370. LS: *Tajomaru in the foreground, the woman cowering in the background.
He backs away from the body and stumbles to the ground in front of the
woman.*

371. MS *of Tajomaru and the woman. They stare over at the body. Tajomaru,
an idiotic expression on his face, rises and takes her hands, but she pulls
them away and begins to back off frantically (pan), ending near the tree
stump in which her husband's sword is still lodged. She utters little*

inarticulate cries. Tajomaru has followed stupidly, and now, half-crazed, he pulls the dead man's sword free and swings it mightily at her as she flees.

372. LS: *she rushes off into the woods; he follows but trips. She disappears as he lies collapsed on the ground.*

373. MS *of Tajomaru's back. He sits up slowly, breathing hard, dirty, sweaty, exhausted. Silence—then the sound of distant cicada.*

374. LS *as he sits stupefied. After a long time, he gets to his feet and goes off, to where the body lies, reappearing a moment later with his own bloody sword as well as the samurai's.*

375. MS: *dragging the swords along, Tajomaru backs off and limps away into the woods.*

376. LS: *the Rashomon gate. The three men sitting, framed overhead by a huge horizontal beam. The sound of the great downpour. The commoner laughs.*

377. MS: *the priest is in the foreground. The commoner stands.*

COMMONER: And I suppose that is supposed to be true.

WOODCUTTER (*getting to his feet*): I don't tell lies. I saw it with my own eyes.

COMMONER: That I doubt.

WOODCUTTER: I don't tell lies.

COMMONER: Well, so far as that goes, no one tells lies after he has said that he's going to tell one.

PRIEST: But it's horrible—if men do not tell the truth, do not trust one another, then the earth becomes a kind of hell.

COMMONER: You are right. The world we live in is a hell.

PRIEST: No. I trust men. (*He turns away from the commoner and rises.*)

378. MCU *of the priest, standing by a column.*

PRIEST: But I don't want to believe that this world is a hell.

The commoner appears behind him, laughing.

COMMONER: No one will hear you, no matter how loud you shout. Just think now. Which one of these stories do you believe?

Before the priest can answer, the woodcutter begins to speak. As he does the camera pans past the column to a MS *of him.*

WOODCUTTER: I don't understand any of them. They don't make any sense.

The commoner steps forward from behind the column and goes up to the woodcutter.

COMMONER: Well, don't worry about it. It isn't as though men were reasonable. (*He turns to walk off.*)

379. LS: *the commoner walks to the fire he has built, squats, and throws several of the burning pieces of lumber out into the rain. Just then the cry of a baby is heard. All look around. The commoner stands up.*

380. MS: *the three men try to locate the source of the crying. Then the commoner runs to the back and heads behind a partition of the gate. The priest and the woodcutter look at each other, then run over to the broken panels of the partition (pan) and peer through to where the woodcutter has disappeared.*

381. MS *from the other side of the partition. The heads of the two men appear through openings in the panels; in the distance, the commoner is kneeling over the baby, stripping off its few clothes.*

382. MS *of the commoner as he finishes removing the clothes and examines them.*

383. MS *of the priest and woodcutter watching; they dash around the partition (pan), the priest picking up the infant and the woodcutter going up to the commoner and pushing him.*

WOODCUTTER: What are you doing?

COMMONER: What does it look like?

384. MCU *of the priest holding the baby protectively.*

385. MS *of the three men, priest in the background, commoner partially hidden by some steps (shot from a low angle).*

WOODCUTTER: That's horrible.

COMMONER: What's so horrible about it? Somebody else would have taken those baby clothes if I hadn't. Why shouldn't it be me?

WOODCUTTER: You are evil.

COMMONER: Evil? Me? And if so, then what are the parents of that baby? (*Pan as he moves up close to the woodcutter.*) They had a good time making it—then they throw it away like this. That's real evil for you.

WOODCUTTER: No, you're wrong. Look! Look here at the amulet case it has on. It's something the parents left to guard over it. Think what they must have gone through to give this baby up.

COMMONER: Oh, well. If you're going to sympathize with other people . . .

WOODCUTTER: Selfish . . .

COMMONER: And what's wrong with that? That's the way we are, the way

we live. Look, half of us envy the lives that dogs lead. You just can't
live unless you're what you call "selfish."

The commoner turns and goes off. The woodcutter moves into MCS *range.*

WOODCUTTER: Brute! (*With gathering anger.*) All men are selfish and
dishonest. They all have excuses. The bandit, the husband . . . you!
(*His face distorted in anger, he leaps in the direction of the commoner.*)

386. MCU *as the woodcutter grabs the commoner by the neck and shakes him;
they struggle out into the rain, and continue to argue there.*

COMMONER: And you say you don't lie! That's just funny. Look, you may
have fooled the police, but you don't fool me.

387. MCU *from reverse angle, the woodcutter facing the camera now. The
commoner's words have affected the woodcutter. Guiltily he lets go his
hold on the commoner.*

388. MCU *from reverse angle. The commoner smiles, then shoves the woodcutter; he comes forward and shoves him again, this time out of frame.
Smiling, the commoner follows him out.*

389. MS *of the two men back under the roof, out of the rain. As the commoner
speaks, he continues to shove the woodcutter back (pan), finally pushing
him against the partition near the priest.*

COMMONER: And so where is that dagger? That pearl-inlay handle that
the bandit said was so valuable? Did the earth open up and swallow it?
Or did someone steal it? Am I right? It would seem so. Now *there* is a
really selfish action for you. (*He slaps the woodcutter and laughs
harshly.*)

390. MCU *of the priest holding the baby.*

391. LS *of all three men.*

COMMONER: Anything else you want to tell me? If not, I think I'll be going.

The baby starts to cry. The commoner glances at it; then, laughing, he turns to go.

392. LS *from outside the gate. The commoner comes out in the rain toward the camera and disappears off-screen. The other two remain under the gate, seen in* LS *through the rain. (Dissolve.)*

393. MS: *the two men, from closer; the sound of the rain diminishes. (Dissolve.)*

394. MS: *the two men, closer yet; rain slowly stopping. (Dissolve.)*

395. MCU: *the two men still standing as before; the sound of the rain has stopped; the baby cries.*

396. LS: *the two men seen from outside the gate as in shot 392, but now the rain has stopped. Drops of water drip from the gate onto the steps. The priest steps forward.*

397. MS: *he walks past the woodcutter, patting the baby, and leaves the frame. The woodcutter stands for a moment, then follows.*

398. MS: *the woodcutter approaches the priest and moves to take the baby away from him; the priest violently resists.*

PRIEST: What are you trying to do? Take away what little it has left?

399. MS: *priest in the foreground. The woodcutter, very humble now, shakes his head.*

WOODCUTTER: I have six children of my own. One more wouldn't make it any more difficult.

400. MS *from reverse angle; woodcutter in the foreground.*

PRIEST: I'm sorry. I shouldn't have said that.

401. MS: *priest in the foreground, as in 399.*

WOODCUTTER: Oh, you can't afford not to be suspicious of people these days. I'm the one who ought to be ashamed. I don't know why I did a thing like that.

402. MS: *woodcutter in the foreground.*

PRIEST: No, I'm grateful to you. Because, thanks to you, I think I will be able to keep my faith in men.

403. MS, *as in 399: priest in the foreground. The woodcutter bows, and the baby, who has been crying all during this dialogue, stops. The priest holds out the baby and the woodcutter takes it. Finale music begins, a distinctly traditional Japanese music.*

404. MS *from farther back. The woodcutter accepts the baby and steps back. The men bow to each other and the woodcutter turns to go.*

405. LS *from behind the men as the woodcutter, holding the infant, leaves the gate; the sky is clear, the priest watches as he goes.*

406. LS *from reverse angle. The woodcutter moves toward the camera. He stops and bows again to the priest. Then he turns and continues on his way, the camera tracking backward with him. The whole gate and the sunny sky come into frame. The woodcutter walks past the camera; the tracking stops and the priest is seen, small, standing under the gate.*

407. *The great signboard of the gate. Music up and out.*

Sources

The Akutagawa Stories

Kurosawa's scenario for *Rashomon* was based on the following two stories, "Rashomon" and "In a Grove," by Ryunosuke Akutagawa (1892-1927). The stories are reprinted here from *Rashomon and Other Stories,* by Ryunosuke Akutagawa, translated by Takashi Kojima (copyright © 1952 by Liveright Publishing Corporation), by permission of Liveright, Publishers, New York.

For a discussion of Kurosawa's use of this source material, see the editor's introductory essay to this volume.

"Rashomon"

It was a chilly evening. A samurai's servant stood under the Rashomon,[1] waiting for a break in the rain.

No one else was under the wide gate. On the thick column, its crimson lacquer rubbed off here and there, perched a cricket. Since the Rashomon stands on Sujaku Avenue, a few other people at least, in sedge hat or nobleman's headgear, might have been expected to be waiting there for a break in the rainstorm. But no one was near except this man.

For the past few years the city of Kyoto had been visited by a series of calamities, earthquakes, whirlwinds, and fires, and Kyoto had been greatly devastated. Old chronicles say that broken pieces of Buddhist images and other Buddhist objects, with their lacquer, gold, or silver leaf worn off, were heaped up on roadsides to be sold as firewood. Such being the state of affairs in Kyoto, the repair of the Rashomon was out of the question. Taking advantage of the devastation, foxes and other wild animals made their dens in the ruins of the gate, and thieves and robbers found a home there too. Eventually it became customary to bring unclaimed corpses to this gate and abandon them. After dark it was so ghostly that no one dared approach.

Flocks of crows flew in from somewhere. During the daytime these cawing birds circled round the ridgepole of the gate. When the sky overhead turned red in the afterlight of the departed sun, they looked like so many grains of sesame flung across the gate. But on that day not a crow was to be seen, perhaps because of the lateness of the hour. Here and there the stone steps, beginning to crumble, and with rank grass growing in their crevices, were dotted with the white droppings of crows. The servant, in a worn blue kimono, sat on the seventh and highest step, vacantly watching the rain. His attention was drawn to a large pimple irritating his right cheek.

As has been said, the servant was waiting for a break in the rain. But he had no particular idea of what to do after the rain stopped. Ordinarily, of course, he would have returned to his master's house, but he had been discharged just before. The prosperity of the city of Kyoto had been rapidly declining, and he had been dismissed by his master, whom he had served many years, because of the

---

1. The "Rashomon" was the largest gate in Kyoto, the ancient capital of Japan. It was 106 feet wide and 26 feet deep, and was topped with a ridgepole; its stone wall rose 75 feet high. This gate was constructed in 789, and in 794 the capital of Japan was transferred to Kyoto. With the decline of Kyoto in the twelfth century, the gate fell into disrepair, cracking and crumbling in many places.—TRANS. [Kojima's note]

effects of this decline. Thus, confined by the rain, he was at a loss to know where to go. And the weather had not a little to do with his depressed mood. The rain seemed unlikely to stop. He was lost in thoughts of how to make his living tomorrow, helpless incoherent thoughts protesting an inexorable fate. Aimlessly he had been listening to the pattering of the rain on the Sujaku Avenue.

The rain, enveloping the Rashomon, gathered strength and came down with a pelting sound that could be heard far away. Looking up, he saw a fat black cloud impale itself on the tips of the tiles jutting out from the roof of the gate.

He had little choice of means, whether fair or foul, because of helpless circumstances. If he chose honest means, he would undoubtedly starve to death beside the wall or in the Sujaku gutter. He would be brought to this gate and thrown away like a stray dog. If he decided to steal . . . His mind, after making the same detour time and again, came finally to the conclusion that he would be a thief.

But doubts returned many times. Though determined that he had no choice, he was still unable to muster enough courage to justify the conclusion that he must become a thief.

After a loud fit of sneezing he got up slowly. The evening chill of Kyoto made him long for the warmth of a brazier. The wind in the evening dusk howled through the columns of the gate. The cricket which had been perched on the crimson lacquered column was already gone.

Ducking his neck, he looked around the gate as he drew up the shoulders of the blue kimono which he wore over his thin undergarments. He decided to spend the night there, if he could find a secluded corner sheltered from wind and rain. He found a broad lacquered stairway leading to the tower over the gate. No one would be there, except the dead, if there were any. So, taking care that the sword at his side did not slip out of the scabbard, he set foot on the lowest step of the stairs.

A few seconds later, halfway up the stairs, he saw a movement above. Holding his breath and huddling cat-like in the middle of the broad stairs leading to the tower, he watched and waited. A light coming from the upper part of the tower shone faintly upon his right cheek. It was the cheek with the red, festering pimple visible under his stubby whiskers. He had expected only dead people inside the tower, but he had gone up only a few steps before he noticed a fire above, near which someone was moving. He saw a dull, yellow, flickering light which made the cobwebs hanging from the ceiling glow in a ghostly way. What sort of person would be making a fire in the Rashomon . . . and in a storm? The unknown, the evil terrified him.

Quietly as a lizard, the servant crept up to the top of the steep stairs. Crouching on all fours and stretching his neck as far as possible, he timidly peered into the tower.

As rumor had said, he found several corpses strewn carelessly about the floor. Since the glow of the light was feeble, he could not count the number. He could only see that some were naked and others clothed. Some were women, and all were sprawled on the floor with their mouths open or their arms outstretched, showing no more sign of life than so many clay dolls. One would doubt that they had ever been alive, so eternally silent were they. Their shoulders, breasts, and torsos stood out in the dim light; other parts vanished in shadow. The offensive smell of these decomposed corpses brought his hand to his nose.

The next moment his hand dropped and he stared. He caught sight of a ghoulish form bent over a corpse. It seemed to be an old woman, gaunt, gray-haired, and nunnish in appearance. With a pine torch in her right hand, she was gazing into the face of a corpse which had long black hair.

Seized more with horror than curiosity, he drew no breath for a time. He felt the hair of his head and body stand on end. As he watched, terrified, she wedged the torch between two floor boards and, laying hands on the head of the corpse, began to pull out the long hairs one by one, as a monkey kills the lice of her young. The hair came out smoothly with the movement of her hands.

As the hair came out, fear faded from his heart, and his hatred toward the old woman mounted. It grew beyond hatred, becoming a consuming antipathy against all evil. At this instant if anyone had brought up the question of whether he would starve to death or become a thief—the question which had occurred to him a little while ago—he would not have hesitated to choose death. His hatred of evil flared up like the piece of pine wood which the old woman had stuck in the floor.

He did not know why she pulled out the hair of the dead. Accordingly, he did not know whether her case was to be judged as good or bad. But in his eyes, pulling out the hair of the dead in the Rashomon on this stormy night was an unpardonable crime. Of course it never entered his mind that a little while ago he had thought of becoming a thief.

Then, summoning strength into his legs, he rose from the stairs and strode, hand on sword, right in front of the old creature. The hag turned, terror in her eyes, and sprang up from the floor, trembling. For a moment she paused, poised there, then lunged for the stairs with a shriek.

"Wretch! Where are you going?" he shouted, barring the way of the trembling hag who tried to scurry past him. Still she attempted to claw her way by. He pushed her back to prevent her. . . . They struggled, fell among the corpses, and grappled there. The issue was never in doubt. In a moment he had her by the arm, twisted it, and forced her down to the floor. Her arms were nothing but skin and bones, and there was no more flesh on them than on the shanks of a chicken. No sooner was she on the floor than he drew his sword and thrust the silver-white blade before her very nose. She was silent. She trembled as if in a fit, and her eyes were open so wide that they were almost out of their sockets, and her breath came in hoarse gasps. The life of this wretch was his now. This thought cooled his boiling anger and brought a calm pride and satisfaction. He looked down at her, and said in a somewhat calmer voice:

"Look here, I'm not an officer of the High Police Commissioner. I'm a stranger who happened to pass by this gate. I won't bind you or do anything against you, but you must tell me what you're doing up here."

Then the old woman opened her eyes still wider, and gazed at his face intently with the sharp red eyes of a bird of prey. She moved her lips, which were wrinkled into her nose, as though she were chewing something. Her pointed Adam's apple moved in her thin throat. Then a panting sound like the cawing of a crow came from her throat:

"I pull the hair . . . I pull out the hair . . . to make a wig."

Her answer banished the unknown from their encounter and brought disappointment. Suddenly she was merely a trembling old woman there at his feet. A ghoul no longer: only a hag who makes wigs from the hair of the dead—to sell, for scraps of food. A cold contempt seized him. Fear left his heart, and his former hatred returned. These feelings must have been sensed by the other. The old creature, still clutching the hair she had pulled from the corpse, mumbled out these words in her harsh broken voice:

"Indeed, making wigs out of the hair of the dead may seem a great evil to you, but these that are here deserve no better. This woman, whose beautiful black hair I was pulling, used to sell dried snake flesh at the guard barracks, saying that it was dried fish. If she hadn't died of the plague, she'd be selling it now. The guards liked to buy from her, and used to say her fish was tasty. What she did couldn't be wrong, because if she hadn't, she would have starved to death. There was no other choice. If she knew I had to do this in order to live, she probably wouldn't care."

He sheathed his sword, and with his left hand on its hilt, he listened to her meditatively. His right hand touched the big pimple on his cheek. As he listened, a certain courage was born in his heart—the courage he had not had when he sat under the gate a little while ago. A strange power was driving him in the opposite direction from the courage he had had when he seized the old woman. No longer did he wonder whether he should starve to death or become a thief. Starvation was so far from his mind that it was the last thing that would have entered it.

"Are you sure?" he asked in a mocking tone, when she finished talking. He took his right hand from his pimple, and, bending forward, seized her by the neck and said sharply:

"Then it's right if I rob you. I'd starve if I didn't."

He tore her clothes from her body and kicked her roughly down on the corpses as she struggled and tried to clutch his leg. Five steps, and he was at the top of the stairs. The yellow clothes he had wrested from her were under his arm, and in a twinkling he had rushed down the steep stairs into the abyss of night. The thunder of his descending steps pounded in the hollow tower, and then it was quiet.

"In a Grove"

The Testimony of a Woodcutter Questioned by a High Police Commissioner

Yes, sir. Certainly, it was I who found the body. This morning, as usual, I went to cut my daily quota of cedars, when I found the body in a grove in a hollow in the mountains.

The exact location? About 150 yards off the Yamashina stage road. It's an out-of-the-way grove of bamboo and cedars.

The body was lying flat on its back dressed in a bluish silk kimono and a wrinkled headdress of the Kyoto style. A single sword stroke had pierced the breast. The fallen bamboo blades around it were stained with bloody blossoms.

No, the blood was no longer flowing. The wound had dried up, I believe. And also, a gadfly was stuck fast there, hardly noticing my footsteps.

You ask me if I saw a sword or any such thing? No, nothing, sir. I found only a rope at the foot of a cedar nearby. And . . . well, in addition to a rope, I found a comb. That was all. Apparently he must have made a battle of it before he was murdered, because the grass and fallen bamboo blades had been trampled down all around.

A horse was nearby? No, sir. It's hard enough for a man to enter, let alone a horse.

The Testimony of a Traveling Buddhist Priest Questioned by a High Police Commissioner

The time? Certainly, it was about noon yesterday, sir. The unfortunate man was on the road from Sekiyama to Yamashina. He was walking toward Sekiyama with a woman accompanying him on horseback, who I have since learned was his wife. A scarf hanging from her head hid her face from view. All I saw was the color of her clothes, a lilac-colored suit. Her horse was a sorrel with a fine mane.

The lady's height? Oh, about four feet five inches. Since I am a Buddhist priest, I took little notice about her details. Well, the man was armed with a sword as well as a bow and arrows. And I remember that he carried some twenty-odd arrows in his quiver.

Little did I expect that he would meet such a fate. Truly, human life is as evanescent as the morning dew or a flash of lightning. My words are inadequate to express my sympathy for him.

The Testimony of a Policeman Questioned by a High Police Commissioner

The man that I arrested? He is a notorious brigand called Tajomaru. When I arrested him, he had fallen off his horse. He was groaning on the bridge at Awataguchi.

The time? It was in the early hours of last night. For the record, I might say that the other day I tried to arrest him, but unfortunately he escaped. He was wearing a dark-blue silk kimono and a large plain sword. And, as you see, he got a bow and arrows somewhere.

You say that this bow and these arrows look like the ones owned by the dead man? Then Tajomaru must be the murderer. The bow wound with leather strips, the black lacquered quiver, the seventeen arrows with hawk feathers—these were all in his possession, I believe.

Yes, sir, the horse is, as you say, a sorrel with a fine mane. A little beyond the stone bridge I found the horse grazing by the roadside, with his long rein dangling. Surely there is some providence in his having been thrown by the horse.

Of all the robbers prowling around Kyoto, this Tajomaru has brought the most grief to the women in town. Last autumn a wife who came to the mountain behind the Pindora of the Toribe Temple, presumably to pay a visit, was murdered, along with a girl. It has been suspected that it was his doing. If this criminal murdered the man, you cannot tell what he may have done with the man's wife. May it please your honor to look into this problem as well.

The Testimony of an Old Woman Questioned by a High Police Commissioner

Yes, sir, that corpse is the man who married my daughter. He does not come from Kyoto. He was a samurai in the town of Kokufu in the province of Wakasa. His name was Kanazawa no Takehiro, and his age was twenty-six. He was of a gentle disposition, so I am sure he did nothing to provoke the anger of others.

My daughter? Her name is Masago, and her age is nineteen. She is a spirited, fun-loving girl, but I am sure she has never known any man except Takehiro. She has a small, oval, dark-complexioned face with a mole at the corner of her left eye.

Yesterday Takehiro left for Wakasa with my daughter. What a misfortune that things should have come to such a sad end! What has become of my daughter? I am resigned to giving up my son-in-law as lost, but the fate of my daughter worries me sick. For heaven's sake, leave no stone unturned to find her. I hate that robber Tajomaru, or whatever his name is. Not only my son-in-law, but my daughter . . . (Her later words were drowned in tears.)

Tajomaru's Confession

I killed him, but not her.

Where's she gone? I can't tell. Oh, wait a minute. No torture can make me confess what I don't know. Now things have come to such a head, I won't keep anything from you.

Yesterday a little past noon I met that couple. Just then a puff of wind blew, and raised her hanging scarf, so that I caught a glimpse of her face. Instantly it was again covered from my view. That may have been one reason; she looked like a Bodhisattva.[1] At that moment I had made up my mind to capture her even if I had to kill her man.

Why? To me killing isn't a matter of such great consequence as you might think. When a woman is captured, her man has to be killed anyway. In killing, I use the sword I wear at my side. Am I the only one who kills people? You, you don't use your swords. You kill people with your power, with your money. Sometimes you kill them on the pretext of working for their good. It's true they don't bleed. They are in the best of health, but all the same you've killed them. It's hard to say who is a greater sinner, you or me. (An ironical smile.)

But it would be good if I could capture a woman without killing her man. So I made up my mind to capture her, and do my best not to kill him. But it's out of the question on the Yamashina stage road, so I managed to lure the couple into the mountains.

It was quite easy. I became their traveling companion, and I told them there was an old mound in the mountain over there, and that I had dug it open and

---

1. In the Buddhist tradition, a Bodhisattva is worshipped for compassionately refraining from entering nirvana until all other beings have been saved.—ED.

found many mirrors and swords. I went on to tell them I'd buried the things in a grove behind the mountain, and that I'd like to sell them at a low price to anyone who would care to have them. Then . . . you see, isn't greed terrible? He was beginning to be moved by my talk before he knew it. In less than half an hour they were driving their horse toward the mountain with me.

When he reached the grove, I told them that the treasures were buried in it, and I asked them to come and see. The man had no objection—he was blinded by greed. The woman said she would wait on horseback. It was natural for her to say so, at the sight of a thick grove. To tell you the truth, my plan worked just as I wished. So I went into the grove with him, leaving her behind alone.

The grove is only bamboo for some distance. About fifty yards ahead there's a rather open clump of cedars. It was a convenient spot for my purpose. Pushing my way through the grove, I told him a plausible lie that the treasures were buried under the cedars. When I told him this, he laboriously pushed his way toward the slender cedars visible through the grove. After a while the bamboo thinned out, and we came to where a number of cedars grew in a row. As soon as we got there, I seized him from behind. Because he was a trained, sword-bearing warrior, he was quite strong, but he was taken by surprise, so there was no help for him. I soon tied him up to the root of a cedar.

Where did I get a rope? Thank heaven, being a robber, I had rope with me, since I might have to scale a wall at any moment. Of course it was easy to stop him from calling out by gagging his mouth with fallen bamboo leaves.

When I disposed of him, I went to his woman and asked her to come and see him, because he seemed to have been suddenly taken sick. It's needless to say that this plan also worked well. The woman, her sedge hat off, came into the depths of the grove, where I led her by the hand. The instant she caught sight of her husband, she drew a small sword. I've never seen a woman of such violent temper. If I'd been off guard, I'd have got a thrust in my side. I dodged, but she kept on slashing at me. She might have wounded me deeply or killed me. But I'm Tajomaru. I managed to strike down her small sword without drawing my own. The most spirited woman is defenseless without a weapon. At last I could satisfy my desire for her without taking her husband's life.

Yes . . . without taking his life. I didn't want to kill him. I was about to run away from the grove, leaving the woman behind in tears, when she frantically clung to my arm. In broken fragments of words, she asked that either her husband or I die. She said it was more trying than death to have her shame known to two men. She gasped out that she wanted to be the wife of whichever survived. Then a furious desire to kill him seized me.

Telling you in this way, no doubt I seem a crueler man than you. But that's because you didn't see her face. Especially her burning eyes at that moment. As I saw her eye to eye, I wanted to make her my wife even if I were to be struck by lightning. I wanted to make her my wife . . . this single desire filled my mind. This was not simply lust, as you might think. At that time if I'd had no other desire than lust, I surely wouldn't have minded knocking her down and running away. Then I wouldn't have stained my sword with his blood. But the moment I gazed at her face in the dark grove, I decided not to leave without killing him.

But I didn't like to resort to unfair means to kill him. I untied him and told him to cross swords with me. The rope that was found at the root of the cedar is the rope I dropped at the time. Furious with anger, he drew his thick sword. And quick as a wink, he sprang at me ferociously, without speaking a word. I needn't tell you how our fight turned out. The twenty-third stroke . . . please remember this. I'm impressed with this fact still. Nobody under the sun has ever clashed swords with me twenty strokes. (A cheerful smile.)

When he fell, I turned toward her, lowering my bloodstained sword. But to my great astonishment she was gone. I wondered where she had run to. I looked for her in the clump of cedars. I listened, but heard only a groaning sound from the throat of the dying man.

As soon as we crossed swords, she may have run away through the grove to call for help. When I thought of that, I decided it was a matter of life and death to me. So, robbing him of his sword, and bow and arrows, I ran out to the mountain road. There I found her horse still grazing quietly. It would be a waste of words to tell you the later details, but before I entered town I had already parted with the sword. That's my confession. I know that my head will be hung in chains anyway, so give me the maximum penalty. (A defiant attitude.)

The Confession of a Woman Who Has Come to the Shimizu Temple

That man in the blue silk kimono, after forcing me to yield to him, laughed mockingly as he looked at my bound husband. How horrified my husband must have been! But no matter how hard he struggled in agony, the rope cut into him all the more tightly. In spite of myself I ran stumblingly toward his side. Or rather I tried to run toward him, but the man knocked me down. Just at that moment I saw an indescribable light in my husband's eyes. Something beyond expression . . . his eyes make me shudder even now. That instantaneous look of my husband, who couldn't speak a word, told me all his heart. The flash in his eyes was neither anger nor sorrow . . . only a cold light, a look of loathing. More struck by the look in his eyes than by the blow of the thief, I called out in spite of myself and fell unconscious.

In the course of time I came to, and found that the man in the blue silk was gone. I saw only my husband still bound to the root of the cedar. I raised myself from the bamboo blades with difficulty, and looked into his face; but the expression in his eyes was just the same as before.

Beneath the cold contempt in his eyes, there was hatred. Shame, grief, and anger . . . I don't know how to express my heart at that time. Reeling to my feet, I went up to my husband.

"Takehiro," I said to him, "since things have come to this pass, I cannot live with you. I'm determined to die . . . but you must die, too. You saw my shame. I can't leave you alive as you are."

This was all I could say. Still he went on gazing at me with loathing and contempt. My heart breaking, I looked for his sword. It must have been taken by the robber. Neither his sword nor his bow and arrow were to be seen in the grove. But fortunately my small sword was lying at my feet. Raising it overhead, once more I said, "Now give me your life. I'll follow you right away."

When he heard these words, he moved his lips with difficulty. Since his mouth was stuffed with leaves, of course his voice could not be heard. But at a glance I understood his words. Despising me, his look said only, "Kill me." Neither conscious nor unconscious, I stabbed the small sword through the lilac-colored kimono into his breast.

Again at this time I must have fainted. By the time I managed to look up, he had already breathed his last—still in bonds. A streak of sinking sunlight streamed through the clump of cedars and bamboos, and shone on his pale face. Gulping down my sobs, I untied the rope from his dead body. And . . . and what has become of me since, I have no more strength to tell you. Anyway, I hadn't the strength to die. I stabbed my own throat with the small sword, I threw myself into a pond at the foot of the mountain, and I tried to kill myself in many ways. Unable to end my life, I am still living in dishonor. (A lonely smile.) Worthless as I am, I must have been forsaken even by the most merciful Kwannon.[2] I killed my own husband. I was violated by the robber. Whatever can I do? Whatever can I . . . I . . . (Gradually, violent sobbing.)

2. A Bodhisattva (see note 1 above).—ED.

The Story of the Murdered Man, as Told Through a Medium

After violating my wife, the robber, sitting there, began to speak comforting words to her. Of course I couldn't speak. My whole body was tied fast to the root of a cedar. But meanwhile I winked at her many times, as much as to say, "Don't believe the robber." I wanted to convey some such meaning to her. But my wife, sitting dejectedly on the bamboo leaves, was staring at her lap. To all appearances, she was listening to his words. I was racked with jealousy. In the meantime the robber went on with this clever talk, from one subject to another. The robber finally made his brazen proposal. "Once your virtue is stained, you won't get along well with your husband, so won't you be my wife instead? It's my love for you that made me violent toward you."

While the criminal talked, my wife raised her face as if in a trance. She had never looked so beautiful as at that moment. What did my beautiful wife say in answer to him while I was sitting bound there? I am lost in space, but I have never thought of her answer without burning with anger and jealousy. Truly she said, "Then take me away with you wherever you go."

This is not the whole of her sin. If that were all, I would not be tormented so much in the dark. When she was leaving the grove as if in a dream, her hand in the robber's, she suddenly turned pale, and pointed at me tied to the root of the cedar, and said, "Kill him! I cannot marry you as long as he lives." "Kill him!" she cried many times, as if she had gone crazy. Even now these words threaten to blow me headlong into the bottomless abyss of darkness. Has such a hateful thing come out of a human mouth ever before? Have such cursed words ever struck a human ear, even once? Even once such a . . . (A sudden cry of scorn.) At these words the robber himself turned pale. "Kill him!" she cried, clinging to his arms. Looking hard at her, he answered neither yes nor no. . . . But hardly had I thought about his answer before she had been knocked down into the bamboo leaves. (Again a cry of scorn.) Quietly folding his arms, he looked at me and said, "What would you like done with her? Kill her or save her? You have only to nod. Kill her?" For these words alone I would like to pardon his crime.

While I hesitated, she shrieked and ran into the depths of the grove. The robber instantly snatched at her, but he failed even to grasp her sleeve.

After she ran away, he took up my sword, and my bow and arrows. With a single stroke he cut one of my bonds. I remember his mumbling, "My fate is next." Then he disappeared from the grove. All was silent after that. No, I heard someone crying. Untying the rest of my bonds, I listened carefully, and noticed that it was my own crying. (Long silence.)

I raised my exhausted body from the root of the cedar. In front of me there was shining the small sword which my wife had dropped. I took it up and stabbed it into my breast. A bloody lump rose to my mouth, but I felt no pain. When my breast grew cold, everything was as silent as the dead in their graves. What profound silence! Not a single bird note was heard in the sky over this grave in the hollow of the mountains. Only a lonely light lingered on the cedars and the mountain. The light gradually grew fainter, till the cedars and bamboo were lost to view. Lying there, I was enveloped in deep silence.

Then someone crept up to me. I tried to see who it was. But darkness had already been gathering round me. Someone . . . that someone drew the small sword softly out of my breast in its invisible hand. At the same time blood again flowed into my mouth. And once and for all I sank down into the darkness of space.

An Autobiographical Account

Something Like an Autobiography

Akira Kurosawa

What follows is excerpted from Kurosawa's *Something Like an Autobiography,* translated by Audie E. Bock (New York: Alfred A. Knopf, 1982), the director's record of his life up to the time of *Rashomon.*

Note that the translator, except for Kurosawa's own name in authorial ascription, follows the Japanese usage of placing the family name first (thus Mifune Toshiro, Kyo Machiko, Miyagawa Kazuo, etc.).

During that time the gate was growing larger and larger in my mind's eye. I was location-scouting in the ancient capital of Kyoto for *Rashomon,* my eleventh-century period film. The Daiei management was not very happy with the project. They said the content was difficult and the title had no appeal. They were reluctant to let the shooting begin. Day by day, as I waited, I walked around Kyoto and the still more ancient capital of Nara a few miles away, studying the classical architecture. The more I saw, the larger the image of the Rashomon gate became in my mind.

At first I thought my gate should be about the size of the entrance gate to Toji Temple in Kyoto. Then it became as large as the Tengaimon gate in Nara, and finally as big as the main two-story gates of the Ninnaji and Todaiji temples in Nara. This image enlargement occurred not just because I had the opportunity to see real gates dating from that period, but because of what I was learning, from documents and relics, about the long-since-destroyed Rashomon gate itself.

"Rashomon" actually refers to the Rajomon gate; the name was changed in a

Noh[1] play written by Kanze Nobumitsu. "Rajo" indicates the outer precincts of the castle, so "Rajomon" means the main gate to the castle's outer grounds. The gate for my film *Rashomon* was the main gate to the outer precincts of the ancient capital—Kyoto was at that time called "Heian-Kyo." If one entered the capital through the Rajomon gate and continued due north along the main thoroughfare of the metropolis, one came to the Shujakumon gate at the end of it, and the Toji and Saiji temples to the east and west, respectively. Considering this city plan, it would have been strange had the outer main gate not been the biggest gate of all. There is tangible evidence that it in fact was: the blue roof tiles that survive from the original Rajomon gate show that it was large. But, no matter how much research we did, we couldn't discover the actual dimensions of the vanished structure.

As a result, we had to construct the *Rashomon* gate to the city based on what we could learn from looking at extant temple gates, knowing that the original was probably different. What we built as a set was gigantic. It was so immense that a complete roof would have buckled the support pillars. Using the artistic device of dilapidation as an excuse, we constructed only half a roof and were able to get away with our measurements. To be historically accurate, the imperial palace and the Shujakumon gate should have been visible looking north through our gate. But on the Daiei back lot such distances were out of the question, and even if we had been able to find the space, the budget would have made it impossible. We made do with a cut-out mountain to be seen through the gate. Even so, what we built was extraordinarily large for an open set.

When I took this project to Daiei, I told them the only sets I would need were the gate and the tribunal courtyard wall where all the survivors, participants, and witnesses of the rape and murder that form the story of the film are questioned. Everything else, I promised them, would be shot on location. Based on this low-budget set estimate, Daiei happily took on the project.

Later Kawaguchi Matsutaro, at that time a Daiei executive, complained that they had really been fed a line. To be sure, only the gate set had to be built, but for the price of that one mammoth set they could have had over a hundred ordinary sets. But, to tell the truth, I hadn't intended so big a set to begin with. It was

---

1. The Noh plays are the classical drama of Japan. Less well-known in the West than the later and more popularly oriented Kabuki dramas, the Noh in their compression and subtlety have exerted a greater influence on Kurosawa; see Donald Richie, *The Films of Akira Kurosawa*, Revised Edition (Berkeley: University of California Press, 1984), p. 117.—ED.

while I was kept waiting all that time that my research deepened and my image of the gate swelled to its startling proportions.

When I had finished *Scandal* for the Shochiku studios, Daiei asked if I wouldn't direct one more film for them. As I cast about for what to film, I suddenly remembered a script based on the short story "Yabu no naka" ("In a Grove") by Akutagawa Ryunosuke. It had been written by Hashimoto Shinobu, who had been studying under director Itami Mansaku. It was a very well-written piece, but not long enough to make into a feature film. This Hashimoto had visited my home, and I talked with him for hours. He seemed to have substance, and I took a liking to him. He later wrote the screenplays for *Ikiru* (1952) and *Shichinin no samurai* (*Seven Samurai*, 1954) with me. The script I remembered was his Akutagawa adaptation called "Male-Female."

Probably my subconscious told me it was not right to have put that script aside; probably I was—without being aware of it—wondering all the while if I couldn't do something with it. At that moment the memory of it jumped out of one of those creases in my brain and told me to give it a chance. At the same time I recalled that "In a Grove" is made up of three stories, and realized that if I added one more, the whole would be just the right length for a feature film. Then I remembered the Akutagawa story "Rashomon." Like "In a Grove," it was set in the Heian period (794-1184). The film *Rashomon* took shape in my mind.

Since the advent of the talkies in the 1930s, I felt, we had misplaced and forgotten what was so wonderful about the old silent movies. I was aware of the esthetic loss as a constant irritation. I sensed a need to go back to the origins of the motion picture to find this peculiar beauty again; I had to go back into the past.

In particular, I believed that there was something to be learned from the spirit of the French avant-garde films of the 1920s. Yet in Japan at this time we had no film library. I had to forage for old films, and try to remember the structure of those I had seen as a boy, ruminating over the esthetics that had made them special.

Rashomon would be my testing ground, the place where I could apply the ideas and wishes growing out of my silent-film research. To provide the symbolic background atmosphere, I decided to use the Akutagawa "In a Grove" story, which goes into the depths of the human heart as if with a surgeon's scalpel, laying bare its dark complexities and bizarre twists. These strange impulses of the human heart would be expressed through the use of an elaborately fashioned play of light and shadow. In the film, people going astray in the thicket of their hearts would wander into a wider wilderness, so I moved the setting to a large forest. I selected the virgin forest of the mountains surrounding Nara, and the forest belonging to the Komyoji temple outside Kyoto.

There were only eight characters, but the story was both complex and deep. The script was done as straightforwardly and briefly as possible, so I felt I should be able to create a rich and expansive visual image in turning it into a film. Fortunately, I had as cinematographer a man I had long wanted to work with, Miyagawa Kazuo; I had Hayasaka to compose the music and Matsuyama as art director. The cast was Mifune Toshiro, Mori Masayuki, Kyo Machiko, Shimura Takashi, Chiaki Minoru, Ueda Kichijiro, Kato Daisuke and Honma Fumiko; all were actors whose temperaments I knew, and I could not have wished for a better line-up. Moreover, the story was supposed to take place in summer, and we had, ready to hand, the scintillating midsummer heat of Kyoto and Nara. With all these conditions so neatly met, I could ask nothing more. All that was left was to begin the film.

However, one day just before the shooting was to start, the three assistant directors Daiei had assigned me came to see me at the inn where I was staying. I wondered what the problem could be. It turned out that they found the script baffling and wanted me to explain it to them. "Please read it again more carefully," I told them. "If you read it diligently, you should be able to understand it because it was written with the intention of being comprehensible." But they wouldn't leave. "We believe we have read it carefully, and we still don't understand it at all; that's why we want you to explain it to us." For their persistence I gave them this simple explanation:

Human beings are unable to be honest with themselves about themselves. They cannot talk about themselves without embellishing. This script portrays such human beings—the kind who cannot survive without lies to make them feel they are better people than they really are. It even shows this sinful need for flattering falsehood going beyond the grave—even the character who dies cannot give up his lies when he speaks to the living through a medium. Egoism is a sin the human being carries with him from birth; it is the most difficult to redeem. This film is like a strange picture scroll that is unrolled and displayed by the ego. You say that you can't understand this script at all, but that is because the human heart itself is impossible to understand. If you focus on the impossibility of truly understanding human psychology and read the script one more time, I think you will grasp the point of it.

After I finished, two of the three assistant directors nodded and said they would try reading the script again. They got up to leave, but the third, who was the chief, remained unconvinced. He left with an angry look on his face. (As it turned out, this chief assistant director and I never did get along. I still regret that in the end I had to ask for his resignation. But, aside from this, the work went well.)

During the rehearsals before the shooting I was left virtually speechless by Kyo Machiko's dedication. She came in to where I was still sleeping in the morning and sat down with the script in her hand. "Please teach me what to do," she requested, and I lay there amazed. The other actors, too, were all in their prime. Their spirit and enthusiasm was obvious in their work, and equally manifest in their eating and drinking habits.

They invented a dish called Sanzoku-yaki, or "Mountain Bandit Broil," and ate it frequently. It consisted of beef strips sautéed in oil and then dipped in a sauce made of curry powder in melted butter. But while they held their chopsticks in one hand, in the other they'd hold a raw onion. From time to time they'd put a strip of meat on the onion and take a bite out of it. Thoroughly barbaric.

The shooting began at the Nara virgin forest. This forest was infested with mountain leeches. They dropped out of the trees onto us, they crawled up our legs from the ground to suck our blood. Even when they had had their fill, it was no easy task to pull them off, and once you managed to rip a glutted leech out of your flesh, the open sore seemed never to stop bleeding. Our solution was to put a tub of salt in the entry of the inn. Before we left for the location in the morning we would cover our necks, arms and socks with salt. Leeches are like slugs— they avoid salt.

In those days the virgin forest around Nara harbored great numbers of massive cryptomerias and Japanese cypresses, and vines of lush ivy twined from tree to tree like pythons. It had the air of the deepest mountains and hidden glens. Every day I walked in this forest, partly to scout for shooting locations and partly for pleasure. Once a black shadow suddenly darted in front of me: a deer from the Nara park that had returned to the wild. Looking up, I saw a pack of monkeys in the big trees above my head.

The inn we were housed in lay at the foot of Mount Wakakusa. Once a big monkey who seemed to be the leader of the pack came and sat on the roof of the inn to stare at us studiously throughout our boisterous evening meal. Another time the moon rose from behind Mount Wakakusa, and for an instant we saw the silhouette of a deer framed distinctly against its full brightness. Often after supper we climbed up Mount Wakakusa and formed a circle to dance in the moonlight. I was still young and the cast members were even younger and bursting with energy. We carried out our work with enthusiasm.

When the location moved from the Nara Mountains to the Komyoji temple forest in Kyoto, it was Gion Festival time. The sultry summer sun hit with full force, but even though some members of my crew succumbed to heat stroke, our work pace never flagged. Every afternoon we pushed through without even stopping for a single swallow of water. When work was over, on the way back to the inn we stopped at a beer hall in Kyoto's downtown Shijo-Kawaramachi district. There each of us downed about four of the biggest mugs of draft beer they had. But we ate dinner without any alcohol and, upon finishing, split up to go about our private affairs. Then at ten o'clock we'd gather again and pour whiskey down our throats with a vengeance. Every morning we were up bright and clear-headed to do our sweat-drenched work.

Where the Komyoji temple forest was too thick to give us the light we needed for shooting, we cut down trees without a moment's hesitation or explanation. The abbot of Komyoji glared fearfully as he watched us. But as the days went on, he began to take the initiative, showing us where he thought trees should be felled.

When our shoot was finished at the Komyoji location, I went to pay my respects to the abbot. He looked at me with grave seriousness and spoke with deep feeling. "To be honest with you, at the outset we were very disturbed when you went about cutting down the temple trees as if they belonged to you. But in the end we were won over by your wholehearted enthusiasm. 'Show the audience something good.' This was the focus of all your energies, and you forgot yourselves. Until I had the chance to watch you, I had no idea that the making of a movie was a crystallization of such effort. I was very deeply impressed."

The abbot finished and set a folding fan before me. In commemoration of our filming, he had written on the fan three characters forming a Chinese poem: "Benefit All Mankind." I was left speechless.

We set up a parallel schedule for the use of the Komyoji location and open set of the Rashomon gate. On sunny days we filmed at Komyoji; on cloudy days we filmed the rain scenes at the gate set. Because the gate set was so huge, the job of creating rainfall on it was a major operation. We borrowed fire engines and turned on the studio's fire hoses to full capacity. But when the camera was aimed upward at the cloudy sky over the gate, the sprinkle of the rain couldn't be seen against it, so we made rainfall with black ink in it. Every day we worked in temperatures of more than 85° Fahrenheit, but when the wind blew through the wide-open gate with the terrific rainfall pouring down over it, it was enough to chill the skin.

I had to be sure that this huge gate looked huge to the camera. And I had to figure out how to use the sun itself. This was a major concern because of the decision to use the light and shadows of the forest as the keynote of the whole film. I determined to solve the problem by actually filming the sun. These days it is not uncommon to point the camera directly at the sun, but at the time *Rashomon* was being made it was still one of the taboos of cinematography. It was even thought that the sun's rays shining directly into your lens would burn the film in your camera. But my cameraman, Miyagawa Kazuo, boldly defied this convention and created superb images. The introductory section in particular, which leads the viewer through the light and shadow of the forest into a world where the human heart loses its way, was truly magnificent camera work. I feel that this scene, later praised at the Venice International Film Festival as the first instance of a camera entering the heart of a forest, was not only one of Miyagawa's masterpieces but a world-class masterpiece of black-and-white cinematography.

And yet, I don't know what happened to me. Delighted as I was with Miyagawa's work, it seems I forgot to tell him. When I said to myself, "Wonderful," I guess I thought I had said "Wonderful" to him at the same time. I didn't realize I hadn't until one day Miyagawa's old friend Shimura Takashi (who was playing the woodcutter in *Rashomon*) came to me and said, "Miyagawa's very concerned about whether his camera work is satisfactory to you." Recognizing my oversight for the first time, I hurriedly shouted "One hundred percent! One hundred for camera work! One hundred plus!"

There is no end for my recollections of *Rashomon*. If I tried to write about all of them, I'd never finish, so I'd like to end with one incident that left an indelible impression on me. It has to do with the music.

As I was writing the script, I heard the rhythms of a bolero in my head over the episode of the woman's side of the story. I asked Hayasaka to write a bolero kind of music for the scene. When we came to the dubbing of that scene, Hayasaka sat down next to me and said, "I'll try it with the music." In his face I saw uneasiness and anticipation. My own nervousness and expectancy gave me a painful sensation in my chest. The screen lit up with the beginning of the scene, and the strains of the bolero music softly counted out the rhythm. As the scene progressed, the music rose, but the image and the sound failed to coincide and seemed to be at odds with each other. "Damn it," I thought. The multiplication of sound and image that I had calculated in my head had failed, it seemed. It was enough to make me break out in a cold sweat.

We kept going. The bolero music rose yet again, and suddenly picture and sound fell into perfect unison. The mood created was positively eerie. I felt an icy chill run down my spine, and unwittingly I turned to Hayasaka. He was looking at me. His face was pale, and I saw that he was shuddering with the same eerie emotion I felt. From that point on, sound and image proceeded with incredible speed to surpass even the calculations I had made in my head. The effect was strange and overwhelming.

And that is how *Rashomon* was made. During the shooting there were two fires at the Daiei studios. But because we had mobilized the fire engines for our filming, they were already primed and drilled, so the studios escaped with very minor damage.

After *Rashomon* I made a film of Dostoevsky's *The Idiot* (*Hakuchi*, 1951) for the Shochiku studios. This *Idiot* was ruinous. I clashed directly with the studio heads, and then when the reviews on the completed film came out, it was as if they were a mirror reflection of the studio's attitude toward me. Without exception, they were scathing. On the heels of this disaster, Daiei rescinded its offer for me to do another film with them.

I listened to this cold announcement at the Chofu studios of Daiei in the Tokyo suburbs. I walked out through the gate in a gloomy daze, and, not having the will even to get on the train, I ruminated over my bleak situation as I walked all the way home to Komae. I concluded that for some time I would have to "eat cold rice" and resigned myself to this fact. Deciding that it would serve no purpose to get excited about it, I set out to go fishing at the Tamagawa River. I cast my line into the river. It immediately caught on something and snapped in two. Having no replacement with me, I hurriedly put my equipment away. Thinking this was what it was like when bad luck catches up with you, I headed back home.

I arrived home depressed, with barely enough strength to slide open the door to the entry. Suddenly my wife came bounding out. "Congratulations!" I was unwittingly indignant: "For what?" "*Rashomon* has the Grand Prix." *Rashomon* had won the Grand Prix at the Venice International Film Festival, and I was spared from having to eat cold rice.

Once again an angel had appeared out of nowhere. I did not even know that *Rashomon* had been submitted to the Venice Film Festival. The Japan representative of Italiafilm, Giuliana Stramigioli, had seen it and recommended it to Venice. It was like pouring water into the sleeping ears of the Japanese film industry.

Later *Rashomon* won the American Academy Award for Best Foreign Language Film. Japanese critics insisted that these two prizes were simply reflections of Westerners' curiosity and taste for Oriental exoticism, which struck me then, and now, as terrible. Why is it that Japanese people have no confidence in the worth of Japan? Why do they elevate everything foreign and denigrate everything Japanese? Even the woodblock prints of Utamaro, Hokusai, and Sharaku were not appreciated by Japanese until they were first discovered by the West. I don't know how to explain this lack of discernment. I can only despair of the character of my own people.

Through *Rashomon* I was compelled to discover yet another unfortunate aspect of the human personality. This occurred when *Rashomon* was shown on television for the first time a few years ago. The broadcast was accompanied by an interview with the president of Daiei. I couldn't believe my ears.

This man, after showing so much distaste for the project at the outset of production, after complaining that the finished film was "incomprehensible," and after demoting the company executive and the producer who had facilitated its making, was now proudly taking full and exclusive credit for its success! He boasted about how for the first time in cinema history the camera had been boldly pointed directly at the sun. Never in his entire discourse did he mention my name or the name of the cinematographer whose achievement this was, Miyagawa Kazuo.

Watching the television interview, I had the feeling I was back in *Rashomon* all over again. It was as if the pathetic self-delusions of the ego, those failings I had attempted to portray in the film, were being shown in real life. People indeed have immense difficulty in talking about themselves as they really are. I was reminded once again that the human animal suffers from the trait of instinctive self-aggrandizement.

And yet I am in no position to criticize that company president. I have come this far in writing something resembling an autobiography, but I doubt that I have managed to achieve real honesty about myself in its pages. I suspect that I have left out my uglier traits and more or less beautified the rest. In any case, I find myself incapable of continuing to put pen to paper in good faith. *Rashomon* became the gateway for my entry into the international film world, and yet as an autobiographer it is impossible for me to pass through the Rashomon gate and on to the rest of my life. Perhaps someday I will be able to do so.

But it may be just as well to stop. I am a maker of films; films are my true medium. I think that to learn what became of me after *Rashomon* the most reasonable procedure would be to look for me in the characters in the films I made after *Rashomon*. Although human beings are incapable of talking about themselves with total honesty, it is much harder to avoid the truth while pretending to be other people. They often reveal much about themselves in a very straightforward way. I am certain that I did. There is nothing that says more about its creator than the work itself.

Reviews and
Commentaries

Reviews

The complex history of the reception of *Rashomon* in Japan is dealt with in the final part of the editor's essay in the "Introduction" section above.

The American and English reviews reprinted here reflect a significant range of critical response. Those reviewers—the majority—who reacted favorably to *Rashomon* also tended to express their fascination with the whole phenomenon of Japanese cinema, then largely unknown in the West.

The New York Times

Bosley Crowther

Rashomon, which created much excitement when it suddenly appeared upon the scene of the Venice Film Festival last autumn and carried off the Grand Prize, is, indeed, an artistic achievement of such distinct and exotic character that it is difficult to estimate it alongside conventional story films. On the surface, it isn't a picture of the sort that we're accustomed to at all, being simply a careful observation of a dramatic incident from four points of view, with an eye to discovering some meaning— some rationalization—in the seeming heartlessness of man.

At the start, three Japanese wanderers are sheltering themselves from the rain in the ruined gatehouse of a city. The time is many centuries ago. The country is desolate, the people disillusioned, and the three men are contemplating a brutal act that has occurred outside the city and is preying upon their minds.

It seems that a notorious bandit has waylaid a merchant and his wife. (The story is visualized in flashback, as later told by the bandit to a judge.) After tying up the merchant, the bandit rapes the wife and then—according to his story—kills the merchant in a fair duel with swords.

However, as the wife tells the story, she is so crushed by her husband's contempt after the shameful violence and after the bandit has fled that she begs her husband to kill her. When he refuses, she faints. Upon recovery, she discovers a dagger which she was holding in her hands is in his chest.

According to the dead husband's story, as told through a medium, his life is taken by his own hand when the bandit and his faithless wife flee. And, finally, a humble wood-gatherer —one of the three men reflecting on the crime—reports that he witnessed the murder and that the bandit killed the husband at the wife's behest.

At the end, the three men are no nearer an understanding than they are at the start, but some hope for man's soul is discovered in the willingness of the wood-gatherer to adopt a foundling child, despite some previous evidence that he acted selfishly in reporting the case.

As we say, the dramatic incident is singular, devoid of conventional plot, and the action may appear repetitious because of the concentration of the

From *The New York Times*, December 27, 1951.

yarn. And yet there emerges from this picture—from this scrap of a fable from the past—a curiously agitating tension and a haunting sense of the wild impulses that move men.

Much of the power of the picture—and it unquestionably has hypnotic power—derives from the brilliance with which the camera of director Akira Kurosawa has been used. The photography is excellent and the flow of images is expressive beyond words. Likewise the use of music and of incidental sounds is superb, and the acting of all the performers is aptly provocative.

Machiko Kyo is lovely and vital as the questionable wife, conveying in her distractions a depth of mystery, and Toshiro Mifune plays the bandit with terrifying wildness and hot brutality. Masayuki Mori is icy as the husband, and the remaining members of the cast handle their roles with the competence of people who know their jobs.

Whether this picture has pertinence to the present day—whether its dismal cynicism and its ultimate grasp at hope reflect a current disposition of people in Japan—is something we cannot tell you. But, without reservation, we can say that it is an artful and fascinating presentation of a slice of life on the screen. The Japanese dia-

From *The New York Times,* January 6, 1952.

logue is translated with English subtitles.

———————

The unprecedented experience presented this past holiday of having a Japanese movie turn up as one of the choice films of the year has fired such amazement and interest in this particular neck of the woods that it rates an exclusive contemplation in this first screed of 1952.

Rashomon, the picture in question, was mentioned here briefly last week as this corner's nomination as the past year's best foreign-language film. And before that, the readers of these pages had been made acquainted with it as the out-of-the-blue Grand Prize winner at the Venice Film Festival last fall. Yet none of these notifications has fully or sufficiently conveyed the strange and disturbing fascination of this conspicuously uncommon film. And we have an uncomfortable feeling that this may turn out inadequate, too.

For the character of this picture is difficult to define because of its dissimilarity to all the familiar types of films. Where storytelling in movies is almost exclusively confined to the forward (or backward) development of a formal dramatic plot, the narrative achievement of this picture is evolved from a single episode, with this one episode—an act of violence—looked at from several points of view. And where pure emotional stimulation is the primary purpose of most films, a deep agitation of the think-box is the strange aim of *Rashomon.*

What we have here, to put it briefly, are four eyewitness accounts of an act that took place in a forest in Japan many centuries ago, brought out in the course of the musings of three wanderers reflecting upon the crime. The first account, as illustrated for the audience sitting as judge, is that of a wild and brutal bandit who precipitated the whole thing. This bandit, with characteristic bluster, tells how he cleverly waylaid an innocent city merchant traveling through the forest with his wife; how he tied up the merchant to rob him and then, overcome by lust, ravished the non-reluctant woman before her husband's eyes. After this act, as he tells it, he set the husband free and fought him fairly and squarely for the possession of the now discountenanced wife. In this sword duel he killed the husband, but during it the woman fled.

This is not the wife's story, however. As she recounts the episode, she was the innocent victim of a brutal rape, and her husband's death followed as an accident when he refused to have compassion upon her. Not so in his recollection. Through a medium, the dead husband says that he

made his own quietus when he saw the infidelity of his wife. And, finally, a humble woodchopper, who is one of three trying to fathom the crime, reports that he witnessed the whole thing and that it wound up in a horrible, savage fight brought on by the wife's shameless urging that the bandit kill her spouse.

After pondering this weird act of violence, the three troubled wanderers conclude that man is a frail and selfish creature. But hope is seen at the end when the woodchopper shows humanity toward an abandoned child.

As one can see, this drama—this probing of a single episode—is far from the usual order of the familiar "story" film. The incident recounted is slender, so far as material goes, and, being repeated four times, it tends, by conventional rules, to pall. Indeed, it will pall very quickly for those who are not prepared to abandon their normal expectations of plot development and suspense and find fresh and subtle stimulation in a strange, analytical approach.

For the wonderful thing about this picture—the thing which sets it up as art—is the manifest skill and intelligence with which it has been made by Director Akira Kurosawa, who moves to the top ranks with this job. Everyone seeing the picture will immediately be struck by the beauty and grace of the photography, by the deft use of forest light and shade to achieve a variety of powerful and delicate pictorial effects. Others, more attentive, will delight in the careful use of music (or absence of music) to accompany the points of view. But only the most observant—and the most sensitive—will fully perceive the clever details and devices by which the director reveals his characters, and, in this revelation, suggests the dark perversities of man.

The Saturday Review

Richard Griffith

The release of any good Japanese film in the United States is news; the arrival of a great one is sensational. *Rashomon* is, for my money, a great film, and the mystery is, where did it come from? It breaks entirely with Japanese film-making tradition, and its editing structure, camera work, and acting challenge comparison with the outstanding film achievements in any country or period. Its greatest novelty is its story, which is non-national, timeless, and universal. More, it is a story about men and women—about sex—and it results, unless I am very much mistaken, in one of the two or three films ever made for grownups, instead of for kiddies six to sixty.

It concerns a double crime—a rape and a murder—told from four points of view, those of the three participants and of an onlooker. The three involved soften their versions to come off as well as possible in their own eyes as well as those of the court before whom they speak. The onlooker's version is presumably the correct one, although he, too, turns out to have

From *The Saturday Review*, January 19, 1952.

been secretly involved in the horrifying scene which he witnessed and which haunts his conscience. These four complex variations on the same theme are unique for the fluidity of their narration, for the clarity of their interrelationship, and for the suspense they build; the film is an editorial tour de force and dramatically draws attention to this crucial function of the movie director. Certainly no director now at work has a better grasp of structure than the unknown (in the West) Akira Kurosawa, whose many talents merit a more complete description than space permits. Since it is impossible to deal with them all, I focus here on the aspect which I think will interest American audiences most, the acting—or, better, Kurosawa's handling of his players.

The acting in *Rashomon* doesn't resemble that in other Japanese films I have seen, which is chiefly derived from the traditional theatre of Japan. Neither is it like stage or screen acting in the contemporary West. It is more like silent film acting than anything else I can think of, and how people will judge it is anybody's guess. In the 1921 *Tol'able David*, there is a scene in which Ernest Torrence, the villain, prepares to fight the hero. As he nerves himself to the attack, a muscle in his face twitches uncontrollably. When this film is shown nowadays at the Museum of Modern Art, most audiences react to the face-twitching with laughter. They have forgotten—the conventions of present-day acting have made them forget—that under the stress of fear or anger, a man loses control of his nervous system. His pulse pounds, his heart beats faster, adrenalin pumps through him, he is apt to shake and make unintelligible noises. He cannot disguise what he feels. Speech is a method for disguising emotion as well as expressing it, and since dialogue dominates most films today, the ability of silent screen actors to exhibit naked emotion has become a forgotten art which is not even recognized as an art when occasionally resurrected.

Rashomon is a reminder of what it was like at its best, and this is no accident. It is part of the design of the film. The three participants in the murder describe it eloquently in words, but their eloquence is false. Like convicts "playing with the evidence," they dress up their stories to their advantage. But when we see what really happened, verbal narration is abandoned, and the camera speaks as only it can. In this harrowing scene, both elemental and sophisticated, the disguises are stripped away and two men and a woman are revealed to one another in a light none of them can bear. All that has gone before was an attempt to mask that revelation, which is simply that "the human heart is hollow and full of filth." But also this strange, profound film reminds us at the very end the heart can be uplifted by the smallest touch, the most fleeting gesture, of compassion. Whoever Akira Kurosawa is, however he came into his greatness as a film director, it was by more than knowing his lenses and his cameras. He knows how difficult it is to live, how necessary to love.

The Christian Science Monitor

John Beaufort

A strange tale of eighth-century Japan has come to the screen in *Rashomon*, the surprise Japanese entry which won the top award at last summer's Venice Film Festival. Acted in a combination of realistic and traditional styles, the film strikes a Western spectator as strangely fascinating, oddly entertaining, and on occasion powerfully affecting.

Rashomon, which is based on Ryunosuke Akutagawa's novel, *In the Forest,* has heretofore baffled Japanese moviemakers. Director-writer Akira Kurosawa and his brilliant cameraman, Kazuo Miyagawa, solved the story's problems with a boldly simple, essentially visual technique.

Here is the tale of a crime, retold from the viewpoints of three living witnesses and the ghost of a fourth. A firewood dealer who is out in the forest sees a bandit hold up a samurai and his wife, violate the wife, and kill the samurai. The camera's eye is used to record the conflicting versions of the crime as told by the bandit, the

From *The Christian Science Monitor,*
January 2, 1952.

wife, the husband's ghost (who speaks through a medium), and the woodcutter.

The picture undoubtedly gains in impact from this repetitive technique. On the other hand, the repetition itself occasionally tends to become monotonous. The monotony is intensified by the at times heavily mannered and—by most Western standards—exaggerated style and performance.

Yet modern and traditional styles are blended more successfully than one might think possible. The realism of the duel between the bandit and the samurai, for instance, is combined with a certain stylized movement, thus heightening the total effect. (For sheer physical violence, the fight scenes match anything one might encounter in a Hollywood film.) Again, when the wife tells her version of the crime, Machiko Kyo relies heavily on the extravagant sobbing and pliant attitudinizing of traditional Japanese acting.

More than once, *Rashomon* reminds one of the material and technique of Japan's *Kabuki* theater. The figure of the medium, who tells the murdered samurai's story, is a familiar figure from Japan's classic folklore and drama.

A fable quality pervades the film; even the characters are designated simply as the Woman, the Bandit, the Man, the Firewood Dealer, the Priest, the Medium, and the Police. But whatever elements are borrowed from the past reach the spectator through the techniques and technology of the present.

Throughout the trial scenes, the priest and the firewood dealer sit motionless in the background, creating a sense of visually aesthetic perspective. Yet the means of registering the scene is a wide-angle lens with what seems an unusual depth of focus. The witnesses deliver their testimony directly in front of the camera—with the result that the spectator finds himself in the position of judge. It is an effective device. The episodes in the mountainous woodland, particularly the recurrent chases, are beautifully and excitingly photographed.

The sequences at the temple— which provide the framework for the flashback narration—are equally impressive. They are shot amid torrential rain. And when it rains in *Rashomon,* the spectator is treated to nothing short of a deluge. The storm during which the firewood dealer begins his weird account finally subsides. Its end produces the contrasting quietude, the surcease from turmoil and torment for the good deed which restores the priest's badly shattered faith in human decency and truthfulness.

Rashomon is set in ancient Kyoto, and the title refers to the main gate where the story begins and ends. At the time of the action, the city's original splendor had long since been lost, owing to natural disasters, wars, and troublesome times. For Japanese spectators, then, the picture may serve as an ancient fable with a modern application.

It is a question how much of this sort of exotic Oriental fare the unaccustomed Western appetite can absorb. But *Rashomon* undoubtedly deserves attention as an authentic piece of motion picture art, a use of the medium in which traditional material emerges fresh and vivid due to masterful and unusual employment of the film medium.

The New Yorker

John McCarten

The other day, the National Board of Review selected *Rashomon,* a Japanese film, as the best foreign picture of the year. It had previously been awarded some kind of prize at one of those European movie festivals, where accolades are passed around as casually as politicians' cigars. Lest these salutes lead you to think that yet another threat to Hollywood is looming, this time in the Orient, I feel I must tell you that *Rashomon* is a lot more simpleminded than any product of the mysterious East has any right to be, and that before it winds up, with a seedy priest and an unwashed woodsman passing an abandoned baby back and forth in the ruins of a pagoda, it has subjected us to a series of inscrutable variations on a Japanese theme involving the sort of carryings-on that stood Queens Village on its ear when Mr. Gray and Mrs. Snyder were on the loose there.[1]

In this case, the trouble takes place in Kyoto in the eighth century. While guiding his wife through a forest close by, a travelling man (inexplicably dressed in dapper plus-fours) meets up with a bandit, who advises him that he has some hot swords hidden in a nearby glen. Although the bandit keeps jumping around and giggling, the travelling man overlooks these manifest peculiarities, on the ground that a good deal is a good deal. The bandit, however, is a sneak who hasn't any swords at all. What he wants is the travelling man's wife, and suddenly he trusses up the husband and proceeds to rape the lady. When the husband is found stabbed to death, the police have a terrible time discovering just how the deed was done. The bandit swears he did it in a fair fight; the lady says that the bandit ran away before her husband came to grief.

These accounts of the affair are given in flashbacks, which become awfully wearing, since the actors keep wheezing, grunting, gurgling, and falling down. To add to the general air of foolishness, a medium presently turns up and says she's been in touch with Daddy in the beyond. Damned

From *The New Yorker,* December 29, 1951.

---

1. In a lurid and well-publicized 1927 trial in New York, Ruth Snyder and her lover, Charles Gray, were convicted of the murder of Snyder's husband.—ED.

if he doesn't swear he committed suicide. Somehow, all this becomes a conversation piece for the priest and woodsman I mentioned a while back, and also for another character—this one right out of *Fu-Manchu*—who has taken refuge from the rain in the ruined pagoda. When it rains in Kyoto, it really rains, and Akira Kurosawa, who directed *Rashomon,* has seen to it that everybody is half-drowned. He has also seen to it that any time his actors have a chance to give their features a thoroughgoing emotional workout, they are photographed in closeup. Perhaps I am purblind to the merits of *Rashomon,* but no matter how enlightened I may become on the art forms of Nippon, I am going to go on thinking that a Japanese potpourri of Erskine Caldwell, Stanislavski, and Harpo Marx isn't likely to provide much sound diversion.

The Times, London

Whether or not a country truly expresses its national character through the medium of the films it makes is a question which does not admit any decided answer. No American, for instance, would agree that Hollywood reflects the real America, but something, some hint of a country's habits of thinking, some perhaps unconscious reflection of its prejudices and preferences, filters through the lens of the camera to perplex or amuse the foreigner.

There is no doubt at all that *Rashomon*, the Japanese film which won the Grand Prize at the 1951 Venice Festival, perplexes, and the difficulty is where to begin an analysis of the perplexities. The film, to start off with, would seem determined to set its face westward and to borrow some of the Hollywood technique, although not in the matter of under-acting. There is little ritual about it, and even the music does not seem to be distinctively Japanese. The story—the reconstruction, from four different points of view, of a murder committed some 1,200 years ago when Japan was torn by civil war and brigandage was rife—would seem to call for a certain passive, Oriental way of playing; what it gets is a treatment rough, boisterous, and noisy enough to shame the most violent gangster film. Whatever these particular Orientals may be, they are certainly neither silent nor inscrutable. The Nobleman (Masayuki Mori) who spends most of the film either tied up or getting murdered, is, it is true, reasonably quiet, but his wife (Machiko Kyo), once she gets going, cries, screams, and has hysterics in the Ercles vein, while Toshiro Mifune, as the bandit, capers about the screen like a ferocious, demented Puck bellowing with maniacal laughter. Screen fights are normally silent affairs, save for an occasional grunt or so, but the contests between the bandit and the nobleman suggest to the ear a battle between four asthmatic under-trained heavyweights all in the ring at the same time. There are some impressive moments in *Rashomon*—and, obscure though the plot often is, it has pattern and intelligence—and one or two lovely shots of forest scenery, but the general impression is one of confusion and noise.

From *The Times*, London, March 14, 1952.

Commentaries

The essays that follow cover a span of more than thirty years. In that period, *Rashomon,* first experienced as the product of a director and an industry as yet virtually unknown in the West (see Harrington below), has achieved acceptance as one of the masterworks of a universally-known filmmaker and has inspired critical examination from a wide variety of viewpoints. Davidson sees the film in the context of post-War Japanese culture, Tyler in the context of modernist esthetics; McDonald's emphasis is formal, Kauffmann's ethical, Mellen's feminist.

Translated by Elliott Stein. First printed in *Cahiers du Cinéma* (May, 1952) as "*Rashomon* et le Cinéma japonais."

Rashomon and the
Japanese Cinema

Curtis Harrington

ashomon took the Grand Prix at the Venice Festival last August to everyone's surprise, and the international fame of the film has been on the in-
crease ever since. RKO immediately bought the American distribution
rights.

As expected, the film made a good deal of money in New York, and probably
did well in other large American cities. It recently won both the National Board
of Review prize and the Oscar for the best foreign film of the year—the two most
important movie awards in the United States.

This success of *Rashomon* in the United States is most interesting, for it reveals, to one who knows how to read between the lines of praise, a *reluctant*
acceptance of its obvious excellence.

Snobbery will always lead Americans to admire the qualities of a French,
English, even a Swedish film. But when an Oriental country like Japan, whose
customs often shock Americans (as primitive and backward), makes a film which
technically and artistically surpasses the best Hollywood productions, then the
amazed American critics feel uneasy and seek facile explanations based on external influences. For them, *Rashomon* is a Japanese postwar film, thus its excellence must be due to the supervision and assistance supplied by the American
occupiers. Nearly all the American reviews stressed "the strong Hollywood influence in the postwar period" and stated that "the Japanese public has been
spoiled by the polish of American movies which their native pictures cannot
easily approach."

All this is untrue. On the contrary, the Japanese cinema can boast of a rich and
brilliant past, the equal of other countries which gave birth to important film
industries: France, England, the United States, Germany, Italy, Russia, and Swe-
den. Unfortunately, only three or four Japanese films have been seen in the West
during the last thirty years; the treasures of Japanese cinema will remain unknown until a means is found to bring to one of our *Cinémathèques* a great
number of the best Japanese silent and sound films, so that we can accord the
Japanese the place they merit in the history of world cinema.

Most good Japanese films do not have contemporary stories, but, like *Rashomon,* are set in the past. This encourages a liberty and fantasy which prevent their becoming routine.

Japanese culture is rich in legends and fantastic tales that have been freely dipped into as source matter for films. The traditional Japanese drama has strongly influenced Japanese cinema, particularly in matters concerning style, rhythm, and acting. The camera, however, was not statically tied down to the expository methods of the theatre; it was granted freedom of movement from the very beginnings of Japanese cinema. It is significant that the Japanese adopted the screenplay as a cinematographic literary form—essentially a way of thinking directly reflecting a series of physically poetic images. On occasion, the source of inspiration was a novel (as in *Rashomon*) but this only made more evident the existence of a creative tradition easily viable for the needs of the average movie.

In 1950 I saw several recent Japanese films in a movie house at Little Tokyo, a neighborhood in Los Angeles. Japanese films are shown there all year round on double-feature bills—one costume and one modern film together. The audience is composed of Southern California Japanese. The high quality of most of these films was obvious. Some of their appeal to Occidental eyes may be attributable to their exoticism; but Hindu films are just as "exotic" for us, yet most of these are of little worth.

Nearly all the Japanese films I saw were marked by a poetic sense of imagery and rhythm of a quality seen only in the very best work of a few important Western directors; in many cases this was combined with a daring and imaginative use of the medium—fast motion, slow motion, montage shots, etc.

The Japanese were certainly influenced by both American and European cinema. They eclectically borrowed the techniques and gimmicks which aided them to express the subject matter of their films. They have been at it since around 1902, and the early works were closely modeled on Western films. What matters, though, is that a careful absorption of filmic possibilities took place, so that many Japanese films, since well before the war, have been sophisticated in both style and subject matter, and technically successful.

Before examining *Rashomon* in greater detail, let me record a few items in those Japanese films seen in Los Angeles which strongly impressed me. . . .

In *Drunken Angel,* a film set in the lower depths of Tokyo, there is a dream sequence on a foggy beach in which a man finds a white coffin swept in by the tide. He opens it with an axe; a horrible caricature of himself emerges from the coffin, and chases him along the shore. Later on in the same film, two men are seen fighting in a corridor whose walls have been freshly painted. During the struggle, a can of white paint spills over and the pair are transformed into macabre figures covered with the sticky white fluid. *Sanshiro Sugata* (1943), an earlier Kurosawa film, recounts a judo legend. At one point, a fighter has been thrown to the ground during combat. He lies dead in a corner of the room; a window shutter breaks loose and falls near the body, in slow motion. The tension of that moment is broken by a close-up of a screaming woman . . . a piercing cry as she discovers the corpse.

The last part of this film is among the most remarkable sequences I have ever seen: A judo combat is taking place on a high hill beaten by the wind and covered by swaying reeds. In the background, the sky is full of dark twisted clouds passing rapidly. At the beginning of the scene, the men are hidden in the grass, their movements merely indicated by sudden changes on the surface of the reeds. It starts to rain; the reeds are flattened out by the rain—the opponents become clearly visible. Finally, the older man loses footing. Vanquished, he slips down the wet reeds, falls to his death in a ravine.

In all these films, visual poetry is the common element—a keen sense of the cinema's creative possibilities.

These tales do not become stereotyped adaptations for the screen, but are true creations in which camera, actors, sets, and music are combined in a stylized whole. Even in *Drunken Angel,* a modern gangster story set in Tokyo, there is no attempt to borrow from Italian "neorealism"; instead, we have a careful combination of all the elements to obtain certain effects. Another surprise is the great technical quality, especially that of the camera work. . . .

In *Rashomon,* Kurosawa attains a degree of camera mobility perhaps not seen since the "flying cameras" of the U.F.A. period (e.g., *Variety, The Last Laugh).*[1]

The camera achieves a new kind of intimacy—it is so precise in its explorations, so active in its participation in the story, and yet so psychologically exact that although, critically, we may speak of a tour de force, we don't see it—we have been taken in and have become accomplices. The three principal performances work well together; the skill with which different aspects of the characters are presented as we see the story from various points of view is such that it is licit to speak of this film as veritable revelation.

It is unlikely that any Western actor would be capable of the dynamism of

---

1. U.F.A. was the great German film conglomerate of the 1920s. *Variety* was directed by E. A. Dupont, 1925; *The Last Laugh* by F. W. Murnau, 1924.—ED.

Toshiro Mifune's performance as the bandit, a portrait of extraordinary erotic savagery, overflowing with force and vitality.

The film's three main settings each have a dominant style distinguishing them from the others according to the humors of the scenes taking place. Thus, the temple (the main gate of the city of Kyoto) is grey, bathed in a heavy, monotonous rain; the police court, where the confession is made, is photographed in static shots in a courtyard lit by bright sun; the forest where the drama breaks but (thrice in the imagination, once in reality) is seen in a constantly changing light filtered by the leaves, which results in broad daylight in some shots and chiaroscuro in others.

The first three main episodes are accompanied by a musical theme a bit irritating to Western ears (a bolero akin to Ravel's), whereas the fourth episode—deliberately, for it is the final part that is the true story—is accompanied only by natural sounds.

It is interesting to note that the "Westernizing" musical scores in Japanese films are stylistically largely derived from French Impressionist and Postimpressionist music—Debussy, Ravel, Roussel, etc.

The novel from which the script is adapted is the work of a well-known modern writer, often called "the Japanese Hemingway." He committed suicide in 1927, after having declared himself incapable of enduring the moral problems of twentieth-century life. The construction of the story itself—the conflict between truth and untruth—is similar to that of certain plays by Pirandello.

I have not read the novel and am incapable of commenting on any changes the script writers saw fit to make. Whatever they are, the film works beautifully; it is the sort of movie which makes clear to us the freshness and the unique magic of the cinema as a means of artistic expression.

Perhaps *Rashomon*'s success abroad will finally lead to the recognition of the Japanese cinema as one of the world's great national film industries.

Rashomon and the Fifth Witness

George Barbarow

Rashomon is rich as a fruit cake visually, and as nutty in structure. Unevenness, imbalance, and wild chaos characterize it; raucous humor is preceded in it by sensuous beauty and followed by deadly serious hysteria; theatrical scenes are placed side by side with bits of pure cinema; at some moments it is a brilliant whodunit, at others a formless philosophical tract; at its end, this prize-winning Japanese extravaganza is indistinguishable from any of a thousand Sunday School plays available at small fee from Samuel French. But after the beginning and before the end, and even during parts of these parts, *Rashomon* is what all movies ought to be as a minimum requirement for mere existence: It is unashamedly photographic, and so it deserves, these days, the loud acclaim and the popularity it has gained. Kurosawa, the director, takes delight in camera images, and fills ninety minutes of screen time with them. Some are graceful, some sentimental, some abstract, some crude and powerful, some ugly, some sensational, some conventionally dull as the *National Geographic*. But no spectator dares close his eyes once Kurosawa has established his main interest in visual images, for to turn away from one moment would be to risk losing some of the priceless pleasure of motion pictures.

The film begins with a veritable deluge of a rainstorm of such photogenic cascadence that one can hardly recollect wetter water; there follows shortly an excursion into a forest, by a swiftly moving camera, that reveals interlaced dizzy patterns of branches, trunks, brush, and blazing splotches of sunlight. In the forest, there is a truly cinematic encounter of a man and his wife with a bandit, ending in a three-way duel, the conflict being described in four different ways, each purporting to be the account of a different person. The bandit's narration, the longest because it includes the encounter along the forest road, is followed by the wife's version, the husband's, and at last by a woodcutter's story. Interlarded among these highly colored, contradictory, and hence nearly incredible expositions are scenes of verbal argument and explanation at the police station, and

From *The Hudson Review* (Autumn, 1952).

further scenes (during the rainstorm) on the porch of an artistic-looking, half-ruined building, where the woodcutter, a tramp, and a priest discuss What It All Means.

The final and overriding complication is Kurosawa's rampaging camera, essentially a pointless instrument because it points too easily everywhere and anywhere. It is an often brilliant but always unreliable fifth witness that observes each of the others as he talks and as he acts in his own version of the desperate, passionate, and violent episode in the forest. There can be no question of accepting the testimony of the official witnesses, for Kurosawa—like Shaw, Pirandello, Gide, or Sascha Guitry—constantly makes observations that belie the "natural" development of the story, that emphasize the process of the telling in a self-conscious and often irritating manner. These observations are usually photographic: the way the pompous policeman plops into the water, the better to observe at a slightly frightened distance the groaning bandit on the river bank; the way the bandit scratches hurriedly at a louse bite during a deadly sword fight; and the way the medium does too much rolling around on the ground at the expense of more views of the husband preparing himself for suicide. What interests the director in this picture is evidently the employment of whatever good idea he happens to think of, and these improvisations are tossed in without much regard for the entire pattern of the film. Indeed, the picture's pattern is merely fortuitous. Unforgivably theatrical scenes are relieved only by the director's photographic penchant; too much is told verbally; and the panning and traveling shots in the forest, although sensuously pretty, do not clarify the structure of the whole film, and bear not the slightest relation to the theme of the picture, which is moral anarchy.

The theme has been explained very well, much better than the moviemakers have done it, by Parker Tyler, in his essay *How to Solve the Mystery of "Rashomon,"* a pamphlet recently published by Cinema 16, the film society.[1] Mr. Tyler's main point is that the paralyzing shock of the terrifying episode in the forest accounts for the variations in the four narratives by the human witnesses. Each, in a numbed state, struggles to reestablish his own identity and, talking from his emotions, invents a story, not particularly caring whether or not it fits the facts or another's version of them. It follows that all apparent inconsistencies in *Rashomon* are actually consistent, and that the film is a "masterpiece." Mr. Tyler's encomium is ingenious and unabashed, as unabashed as Kurosawa's enthusiasm

---

1. Reprinted below as "*Rashomon* as Modern Art."—ED.

for his camera. But a masterpiece of a film is not confused and not confusing, as *Rashomon* is. It does not, and should not, like *Rashomon,* imitate in a protean manner the anarchy it proposes to reveal. A film ought not to be a hodgepodge or a ragbag, a veritable anthology of narrative styles, especially when the director possesses the fifth witness and does not fully control it. That he does not control it all the time is plain enough from the opening title and from the priest's opening speech: The events to be shown take place in a time of wars, fires, famines, earthquakes, typhoons, a time of death and destruction, hence also a time of moral decay. This stuff is verbal, and verbal stuff carries small conviction on the screen. There should be and could be better evidence that this is a time of disasters, a time when the unnatural becomes natural, when the cultural and social order is shaken to the center. What is needed in the film is cinematic evidence having the cogency of the dramatic evidence in the wonderfully articulate beginnings of *Macbeth* and *Hamlet.* It is all very well to start with an excellent rainstorm, but rain is not an earthquake and a sword fight is not a war, and a moviemaker who must rely on a direct title to make a main point is not a master.

The baby is the worst. At the end, the woodcutter is caught in a lie about his version of the forest episode. The tramp sneers. The priest feels more pain, since his faith in man is already badly damaged. Then a baby's cry is heard. It is a foundling. The tramp steals the baby's rich bedding and then leaves, as he denounces the hypocritical woodcutter for attempting to stop the theft. The latter worthily attempts to take the baby, is rebuffed by the horrified priest, then gets the baby by declaring he will bring it up as one of his own children. The priest having regained his faith, and the bathos having been multiplied unconscionably, the rain stops; and so the picture ends in a cliché so wild that Broadway audiences were able to recognize it as a joke in *Boy Meets Girl: My Gawd!, cries the grizzled prospector as he stumbles over something soft in the snow. My Gawd! A Baby!*[2] Mr. Tyler, embarrassed by the baby, believes "the film would have remained intact without it," but we might ask how the film could have ended much differently, since the theme is expressed not by the action and visual structure of the picture but by a number of stiff and dull verbalisms of the *c'est la guerre* variety.

Such misfortunes reduce the very real pleasure and intense excitement generated by portions of *Rashomon* where sights and actions escape the inhibitions of

2. *Boy Meets Girl* was a 1935 Broadway farce written by Sam and Bella Spewack. In it, two Hollywood screenwriters create a box office success by concocting a sentimental story involving a cowboy and a baby.—ED.

playlet forms, but they cannot completely destroy the vitality of Kurosawa's shots. Even the slowest of "message" scenes can be sat through just by studying the compositional patterns on the screen. And when a sequence is going strong, as in the two sword fights, which are meant to be compared one with the other, the work is magnificent.

Rashomon as Modern Art

Parker Tyler

Rashomon, the Japanese film masterpiece, is a story about a double crime: rape and homicide (or possibly suicide). The time is the eighth century A.D. It is told in retrospect, and in successive layers, by the three participants, the dead warrior (through a mediumistic priestess), his raped wife, and a notorious bandit perhaps responsible for the warrior's death as well as for his wife's violation, and by a woodcutter who alleges himself to have witnessed, accidentally, the whole episode. The quality of the film narrative is so fine that an astonishingly unified effect emerges from the conflicting stories furnished by the three principals and (following the inquest) by the lone witness. The bandit and the woman have separately fled the scene of the crimes, where the woodcutter claims, at first, to have arrived only in time to find the warrior's corpse. Nominally, the film comes under the familiar heading of stories that reconstruct crimes. However, this story does not go much beyond the presentation of each person's testimony.

The woman claims to have killed her husband in an irresponsible fit of horror after the rape took place; her husband claims to have committed hara-kiri out of grief and humiliation; the bandit claims to have killed him in honorable combat; and the woodcutter confirms the bandit's story while picturing the conduct of all participants quite differently from the ways they respectively describe it. As no trial of either of the living participants is shown, and as no consequent action reveals anything conclusive as to the crime, the decision as to the actual truth of the whole affair falls to the spectator's option. Since technically the woodcutter is the only "objective" witness, he might seem the most reliable of the four testifiers. But his integrity is *not* beyond question; the version by the warrior's ghost has contradicted his version in an important detail—one inadvertently confirmed by the woodcutter's implicit admission (in an incident following the inquest) that he stole a dagger at the scene of the crime. The ghost has testified that he felt "someone" draw from his breast the dagger with which he alleges he committed hara-kiri.

Logically, if one's aim be to establish in theory the "legal" truth of the affair,

From *The Three Faces of the Film* (New York: Thomas Yoseloff, 1960).

the only obvious method is to correlate all the admissible facts of the action with the four persons involved, in order to determine their relative integrity as individuals—a procedure complicated necessarily not merely by the given criminal status of one participant but by the fact that all but the woodcutter have willingly assumed guilt. A further difficulty, in general, is that nothing of the background of any character is given beyond what can be assumed from his visible behavior and his social status; for example, there is only the merest hint of something unusual in the journey of the warrior and his lady through the forest. Again, even from direct observation, we have to depend a great deal on these persons as seen through the eyes of each other. So, unless one be prejudiced for one sex or another, one social class or another, it seems almost impossible to make a really plausible choice of the truth-teller (if any). Are we to conclude, in this dilemma, that *Rashomon* amounts to no more than a trick piece, a conventional mystery melodrama, left hanging? My answer is *No*. There are several things about the movie which argue it as a unique and conscious art, the opposite of a puzzle; or at least, no more of a puzzle than those modern paintings of which a spectator may be heard to say, "But what is it? What is it supposed to mean?"

Perhaps more than one profane critic has wisecracked of a Picasso, a Dali, or an Ernst, that it demands, *a posteriori,* the method described by the police as "the reconstruction of the crime." My opinion is that the last thing required for the elucidation of *Rashomon*'s mystery is something corresponding to a jury's verdict. Such a judgment, aesthetically speaking, is as inutile for appreciating the substance of this movie as for appreciating the art of Picasso. In *Rashomon,* there is no strategic effort to conceal any more than a modern painter's purpose is to conceal instead of reveal. The basic issue, in art, must always be *what* the creator desires to reveal. Of such a painting as Picasso's *Girl Before Mirror,* it may be said that it contains an "enigma." But this enigma is merely one specific aspect of the whole mystery of being, a particular insight into human consciousness in terms of the individual, and so has that complex poetry of which all profound art partakes. So with the enigma of *Rashomon.* This great Japanese film is a "mystery story" to the extent that existence itself is a mystery, as conceived in the deepest psychological and aesthetic senses. As applied to a movie of this class, however, such a theory is certainly unfamiliar and therefore has to be explained.

Chagall with his levitated fantasy-world and childhood symbols, Picasso with his creative analysis of psychological movements translated into pictorial vision—such painters set forth *nude* mysteries of human experience; each, in the static field of the painting, reveals multiple aspects of a single reality, whether literally or in symbols. *Rashomon,* as a time art, cinema, corresponds with multiple-image painting as a space art. The simplest rendering of time phases in an object within the unilateral space of a single picture is, of course, in Futurist painting, such as Balla's famous dog, ambling by the moving skirts of its owner; the dachshund's legs are portrayed multiply with a fanlike, flickering kind of image similar to images as seen in the old-fashioned "bioscope" movie machine. The same dynamic principle was illustrated by Muybridge's original time-photography of a running horse, except that the register there was not instantaneous but successive; at least, the photographer had the cinematic idea of keeping pace with a running horse to show the pendulumlike span of its front and hind legs while its body seemed to stay in the same place (treadmill dynamics). Even in the contemporary movie camera, some movements may be so fast that one gets the sort of blur shown in Futurist images. The analogy of *Rashomon* with such procedures of stating physical movement is that, for the single action photographed, a complex action (or "episode") is substituted, and for the single viewpoint toward this action, multiple (and successive) viewpoints. The camera in this movie is actually trained four times on what theoretically is the same episode; if the results are different each time, it is because each time the camera represents the viewpoint of a different person; a viewpoint mainly different, of course, not because of the physical angle (the camera is never meant to substitute for subjective vision) but because of the psychological angle.

"Simultaneous montage" in cinema is the double exposure of two views so that multiple actions occur in a *unilateral space visually* while existing in *separate spaces literally* and possibly—as when a person and his visual recollection are superimposed on the same film frame—also in separate times. A remarkable aspect of the method of depicting memory in *Rashomon* is its simplicity: Each person, squatting in Japanese fashion as he testifies, squarely faces the camera and speaks; then, rather than simultaneous montage, a flashback takes place: the scene shifts wholly to the fatal spot in the forest. The police magistrate is never shown and no questions addressed to the witnesses are heard. When it is the dead man's turn to testify, the priestess performs the required rite, becomes possessed by his spirit, speaks in his voice, and the scene shifts back as in the other cases. Thus we receive the successive versions of the action with little intervention between them and with the minimum of "courtroom action."

Of course, there is a framing story, which retrospectively reveals the inquest itself. The action literally begins at the Rashomon Gate, a great ruin where the woodcutter and the priest, who has previously seen the woman and been present at the inquest, are sheltered during a rainstorm; joined by a tramp, these two gradually reveal everything that has taken place according to the several versions. What is important is the inherent value of the way the technique of the flashback has been variously used. The separate stories are equally straightforward, equally forceful; no matter which version is being related, his own or another's, every participant behaves with the same conviction. As a result (it was certainly this spectator's experience), one is compelled to believe each story implicitly as it unfolds, and oddly none seems to cancel another out. Therefore it would be only from the policeman's viewpoint of wanting to pin guilt on one of the persons that, ultimately, any obligation would be felt to sift the conflicting evidence and render a formal verdict. Despite the incidental category of its form, *Rashomon* as a work of art naturally seems to call for a response having nothing to do with a courtroom.

Of an event less significant, less stark and rudimentary in terms of human behavior, the technical question of "the truth" might prove insistent enough to embarrass one's judgment. The inevitable impulse, at first sight, is to speculate on which of those who claim guilt is really guilty of the warrior's death. But whatever conclusion be tentatively reached, what eventually slips back into the spectator's mind and possesses it is the traumatic violence of the basic pattern: that violence which is the heart of the enigma. The civilization of this medieval period is turned topsy-turvy by the bandit's strategy, in which he tricks the man, ties him up, and forces him to witness his wife's violation. It is only from this point forward that the stories differ: the woman's reaction to the bandit's assault, the husband's behavior after being freed from his bonds—everything is disputed by one version or another. But is not the heart of the confusion *within the event itself*? Is this happening not one so frightfully destructive of human poise and ethical custom that it breeds its own ambiguity, and that this ambiguity infects the minds of these people?

All the participants are suffering from shock: the warrior's agonized ghost, his hysterical wife, the bandit, when caught, seized with mad bravado. Unexpectedly—for the paths of the couple and the bandit have crossed purely by accident—three lives have been irretrievably altered after being reduced to the most primitive condition conceivable. Two men (in a manner in which, at best, etiquette has only a vestigial role) have risked death for the possession of a woman. Basically, it is a pattern that was born with the beginnings of mankind. Such an event, in civilized times of high culture, would of itself contain something opaque and even incredible. What matters morally is not how, from moment to moment, the affair was played out by its actors but that it should have been played *at all*. The illicit impulse springing up in the bandit's breast as the lady's long veil blows aside is so violent that its consequences attack the sense of reality as its moral root. Regardless of what literally took place in the forest's depths that mild summer day, each participant is justified in reconstructing it in a manner to redeem the prestige of the moral sense, which, consciously or not, is a civilized person's most precious possession. It should be emphasized that it is the Japanese people who are involved, and that to them honor is of peculiarly paramount value; even the bandit is quick to seize the opportunity to maintain—truthfully or not—that he behaved like a man of caste rather than an outlaw; he has testified that following the rape (to which, he says, the woman yielded willingly) he untied the husband and worsted him in fair swordplay.

Hence, a psychologically unilateral, indisputable perspective exists in which the tragic episode can be viewed *by the spectator:* a perspective contrary to that in which one of the persons appears technically guilty of the warrior's death. This perspective is simply the catastrophe as a single movement which temporarily annihilated the moral reality on which civilized human consciousness is based. The "legal" or objective reality of the affair (what might be called its *statistics*) is exactly what cannot be recovered, because the physical episode, as human action, has been *self-annihilating*. Of course, then, it might be claimed that the woodcutter, not being involved except as a spectator, is a disinterested witness of the episode, and accordingly his story that the three actors in the tragedy really played a grim farce, in which two cowards were the heroes and a shrew the heroine, is the correct version. But the opening scene of the framing story makes it plain that the woodcutter's mind is in a state similar to that of the participants themselves; indeed, he is evidently dismayed and apparently by the fact that all their testimony belies what he proceeds to reveal to the priest and the tramp as "the truth." However, as the shocked witness of such a debacle of the social order—in any case a victory of evil over good—this peasant may have withheld his testimony out of superstitious timidity. If, in fact, he saw all that took place, then the added confusion that the participants contradict each other may raise bewilderment in his simple mind—may even tempt him to exploit his subconscious envy and resentment against his betters by imagining their behavior as disgraceful and ludicrous. It seems within *Rashomon*'s subtle pattern to suggest that even a simple, disinterested witness should be drawn psychologically into the chaos of this incident; after all, there is no proof that he did not invent his own account in competition with the others. This assumption would lend credit to the conclusion that the real function of each witness's story is to salvage his own sense of reality, however close his version to the event as it took place. Perhaps it would be accurate to add that the facts themselves have no true legal status, since each witness is forced to draw on his subjective imagination rather than on his capacity to observe. In this case, each is in the position of the proto-artist, who uses reality only as a crude norm; the sense of invention enters *into* reality. On the other hand, there is the literal truth of denouement, the climax of the framing story, in which the woodcutter adopts a foundling baby who has been left in the Gate's interior. The relation of this incident to the story proper strikes me as the most problematical element of all, if only because the film would have remained intact without it.

Morally, of course, this incident functions as a reinstatement of human values in the sense of good. But the specifically religious view that humanity has hopelessly degraded itself in the forest episode (the view represented by the priest) is more external than essential to the whole conception. The priest thinks in terms equivalent, logically, to the law's terms: truth or falsehood. Since some lying is self-evident, the sin of concealment is added to crime; i.e., concealment of the truth, not of the crime, for all profess crime. Ironically enough, *confession* has become a sin. What seems significant to the whole is the collective nature of the liars: they literally outnumber the truth-teller (whichever he may be). The "sin" involved has gone beyond individual performance and exists objectively, as would a natural cataclysm such as a volcanic eruption. That each participant assumes guilt, including the dead man, reveals the comprehensiveness and irresistibility of the disorder. A lie, then, actually becomes the symbol of the operation by which these people mutually regain their moral identities. These identities having been destroyed as though by an objective force beyond anyone's control, any means seems fair to regain them. Since, however, they cannot separate themselves from the sense of *tragedy,* they prefer to be tragedy's heroes—its animating will rather than its passive objects. But why should the three tragedies seem as one?

To revert to our analogy with the visual media of painting and still photography, the plastic reality with which we have to deal in *Rashomon* is multiform rather than uniform. Within one span of time-and-space, reality (the episode in the forest) has been disintegrated. While the witnesses' stories accomplish its reintegration, they do not do so in terms of the *physically unilateral* except in the final aesthetic sense in which the totality of a work exists all at once in a spectator's mind. The analogy is complex, but literally it is with the Futuristic image of the walking dog; like this image, the total image of *Rashomon* varies only in detail and degree. There is no variation on the background and origin of the tragedy; no contradiction as to the main physical patterns of the rape and the death of the warrior by a blade wound. So the main visual aspect is held firmly, unilaterally, in place. Another image of Futurist painting renders the angles of air displacement caused by the nose of a racing auto. Such "displacements" exist in *Rashomon* severally in the respective accounts of a physical action deriving from one main impetus: the desire to possess a woman.

The total psychological space in this movie, because of its complexity, is rendered in literal time as is music. A similar psychological space is rendered *simultaneously* in Picasso's *Girl Before Mirror* by the device of the mirror as well as by the double image of profile-and-fullface on the girl. Her moonlike face has a symbolic integralness as different "phases" of the same person; that is, her fullface denotes her personality as it confronts the world and her profile her personality as it confronts itself: the mirror image in which the fullface character of her aspect is diminished. To Meyer Schapiro we owe a basic observation as to this painting: It plays specifically on the body-image which each individual has of himself and others, and which is distinct from the anatomical image peculiarly available to photography. The mirror image in Picasso's work thus asserts a psychological datum parallel with the dominantly subjective testimony of each witness in *Rashomon*'s tragedy. The mirror of the movie screen is like the mirror in the painting as telescoped within the image of the total painting; successively, we see people as they think of themselves and as they are to others; for example, at one point during the woman's story, the camera substitutes for the viewpoint of her husband toward whom she lifts a dagger: We see her as conceived by herself but also as she would have been in her husband's eyes. In revealing, with such expressiveness and conviction, what novels have often revealed through first-person narratives or the interior monologue, the film necessarily emphasizes its *visual* significance. The sum of these narratives in *Rashomon* rests on the elements of the tragedy in which all agree: One raped, one was raped, one killed, one was killed. The "variations" are accountable through something which I would place parallel with Schapiro's body-image concept: the *psychic image* that would apply especially to the memory of a past event in which the body-image is charged with maintaining, above all, its moral integrity, its ideal dignity. In a sense, Picasso's girl reconstructs and synthesizes her outer self-divisions within the depths of the mirror; so in the depths of each person's memory, in *Rashomon,*

is recreated the image of what took place far away in the forest as consistent with
his ideal image of himself.

In modern times, the human personality—as outstandingly demonstrated in
the tragicomedies of Pirandello—is easily divided against itself. But what makes
a technically schizophrenic situation important and dramatically interesting is,
paradoxically, the individual's sense of his former or possible unity, for without
this sense he would not struggle morally against division: he would be satisfied to
be "more than one person." In analytical cubism, we have a pictorial style expressing an ironic situation within the human individual's total physique, including his clothes; we do not perceive, within an individual portrayed by Picasso in
this manner, a moral "split" or psychological "confusion"; rather we see the
subject's phenomenal appearance portrayed formalistically in terms of its internal or "depth" elements, its overlaid facets, or complex layers of being, which—
though presumably not meant to signify a conflict in the personality—correspond logically, nevertheless, to the moral dialectic within all consciousness
(subjective/objective, personal/social, and so on). The same logical correspon-
dence is seen even more plainly in the anatomical dialectic of Tchelitchew's recent paintings, where the separate inner systems are seen in labyrinthine relation
to the skin surface. Indeed, man as an internal labyrinth is common to diverse
styles of modern painting, all such styles necessarily implying, as human statements, the sometimes bewildering complexity of man's spiritual being. Great
beauty is justifiably found in such aesthetic forms, which indirectly symbolize an
ultimate mystery: that *human* mystery to which *Rashomon* so eloquently testifies
in its own way and which comprises the transition from birth to death, from the
organic to the inorganic, which is the individual's necessary material fate.

Against the awareness of his material fate, the individual erects many de-
fenses: art, pleasure, ethics, God, religion, immortality—ideas, sensations, and
acts whose continuity in him are preserved by constant cultivation, periodic re-
newal, unconscious "testimony." These constitute his moral identity in the social
order. In them resides the essence of his being, the law of his contentment (such
as it be), and his rational ability to function from hour to hour. In the lives of the
persons of *Rashomon*, where this objective order prevailed, utter chaos was suddenly injected. Each person was shaken out of himself, became part of that blind
flux which joins the intuition of the suspense-before-birth with that of the
suspense-before-death and whose name is terror. This was largely because of the
tragedy's physical violence, which temporarily vanquished human reason. If we
look at the terror of war as depicted in Picasso's *Guernica,* we observe a social

cataclysm of which the forest episode in *Rashomon* is a microcosm. Curiously enough, *Guernica* happens to be divided vertically into four main sections, or panels, which Picasso has subtly unified by overlapping certain formal elements. Thus, while the great massacre is of course highly simplified here in visual terms, it is moreover synthesized by means of four stages or views. As wrenched by violence as are the individual forms, they congregate, so to speak, to make order out of confusion. Though Picasso was not recomposing from memory, he might have been; in any case, the drive of art is toward formal order, and the individuals in *Rashomon,* as proto-artists, have this same drive. As gradually accumulated, the sum total of *Rashomon* constitutes a *time mural* whose unity lies in the fact that, however different are the imaginations of the four witnesses, whatever harsh vibrations their mutual contradictions set up, the general design (as the filmmakers have molded it) remains and dominates the work's final aspect of great beauty and great truth.

Memory of Defeat in Japan:
A Reappraisal of *Rashomon*

James F. Davidson

The signing of the military-aid pact between the United States and Japan early this year formally marked the opening of a new phase in the relationship between the two countries and an end to the interlude of the "Switzerland of the Pacific." It signified the American desire to see the country so recently known as a defeated enemy and devastated dependent become an increasingly self-sufficient and dependable ally.

Outcroppings of anti-Americanism in Japan since the end of the occupation have been of the type that could be expected in the period of readjustment, with the Japanese reactions to the hydrogen bomb tests adding a special sort of tension. The underlying attitudes are the real point of concern, and these should have more attention in the future than Americans have been accustomed over the past few years to give to Japanese opinion. The attitude of an ally both deserves and requires a different quality of understanding than is accorded to a subdued enemy.

As a particular insight into Japanese feelings, it is worth taking another look at the most widely acclaimed of Japan's dramatic products since the war, the origin of which dates well back into the occupation period. It is now more than two years since the film *Rashomon* was first seen by New York audiences after having won the Grand Prize at the International Film Festival in Venice. It was subsequently shown in many American cities and won critics' citations as an outstanding foreign film. The purpose of this review is to point out some implications of *Rashomon* in terms of the Japanese reflection on their defeat and occupation which were completely overlooked by American reviews at the time. These overtones are present throughout the picture and come through strongly in many of its details. Without producing a consistent theme, they heighten the dramatic effect of the story upon a Japanese audience in a way which is easily lost upon the foreign observer.

The story is laid in the ancient capitol of Kyoto, during a troubled period in the ninth century. It concerns a samurai and his wife waylaid on the road by a

From *The Antioch Review* (December, 1954).

notorious bandit. The man is killed and the woman flees, later seeking refuge in a temple whence she is brought to the police magistrate after the capture of the bandit. A woodcutter who found the body and a Buddhist priest who passed the couple on the day of the crime are present at the testimony. As the picture opens, these two relate the events to a stranger while the three seek shelter from the rain in the ruins of the great gate of Kyoto, the Rashomon.

The bandit, Tajomaru, boasted that he had slain the man. Catching a glimpse of the woman as the couple passed him on the road, he had resolved to possess her, and, if possible, to do so without killing her husband. With a tale of swords and mirrors buried near an abandoned temple, he enticed the man into the woods, where he overcame and bound him. On being led to the spot, the wife attacked the bandit with a dagger, fighting like a tigress until at last, exhausted and hysterical, she not only succumbed but finally returned his embrace.

Afterwards, as he was about to leave, she stopped him, saying that she could not stand disgrace in the eyes of two men. One must die, and she belong to the other. He released the husband and they fought. After the samurai had won the bandit's admiration by crossing swords with him longer than any previous foe, he was slain. Finding the woman gone, the bandit took the horse and weapons, except for the dagger, which he forgot. He was apprehended shortly after, writhing ignominiously with stomach cramps as a result of drinking from a polluted stream.

According to the wife, the bandit left after the attack, laughing derisively. She ran to her husband to find nothing but contempt in his eyes, even when she cut his ropes and begged him to kill her. Maddened by his stare, she approached with the dagger, fainted, and recovered to find that she had plunged it into his chest.

Next, in a procedure which modern homicide squads must contemplate wistfully, the testimony of the dead man is obtained through a medium. He says that the bandit urged his wife to go with him, declaring his love and saying that her husband would not want her now. To his horror, she not only consented, but as they left she pulled the bandit back and cried, "Kill him!" The bandit stared at her in unbelief and then said to her husband, "Shall we kill her, or let her go? You decide." For that, says the dead man, he could almost forgive him. As he hesitated, she wrenched free and fled. After a chase, the bandit returned alone, cut his ropes, and left. He rose, sobbing, found the dagger and killed himself. As he lost consciousness, he was aware of someone approaching and drawing out the dagger.

At this point in the film, the stranger laughs at the discomfort of the two narrators. The priest is miserable because the same faith that requires him to believe the dead man's story is shaken by the account of the woman's treachery. The woodcutter suddenly bursts out that he knows the man was killed with a sword because he saw it happen. He concealed his knowledge from the police out of a desire not to be involved. Coming upon the clearing, he had seen the man bound and the bandit entreating the woman. Finally, she ran to her husband, cut his ropes, and threw herself on the ground halfway between the men. The bandit drew, but the husband refused to risk his life for her, saying, "I regret the loss of my horse more." The bandit considered a moment, then turned to leave and rebuffed the woman as she ran after him.

She began to laugh wildly and denounced both of them. She had long been sick of "this farce," indicating her husband, and had been thrilled to learn the identity of her attacker. Perhaps Tajomaru was a way out for her. But no! He did not take her like a conqueror. She told her husband that he could hardly sneer at her honor if he was too poor a specimen to fight for her. Goaded by her, they fought unwillingly, unskillfully, even cravenly. It was not a duel; it was a terrified brawl. At last the husband was trapped in the undergrowth and, shouting that he did not want to die, was run through. The staggering, panting Tajomaru returned to the woman, who had watched in horrified fascination. She fought him off and fled. He then gathered up both swords and left.

When the woodcutter has finished his account, the stranger again laughs at the unhappiness of the other two over this exposure of human frailty and deceit. "Men want to forget things they don't like," he says. These three now become principals in the epilogue, which is very important to an understanding of the film. They hear a cry and discover an abandoned baby around a corner of the gate. The stranger, who reaches it first, strips the blankets from it. The horrified priest takes the baby while the woodcutter seizes the stranger and denounces him as the incarnation of evil. He justifies himself, saying that the parents have abandoned their duty and he is not obliged to take it up. Everyone must live any way he can, and if he does not steal the blankets someone else will. Still pressed by the woodcutter, he rebounds with the taunt that he knows why the last story was concealed from the police. He accuses the woodcutter of having taken the dagger, described by the bandit as valuable, from the scene of the crime. The crestfallen woodcutter makes no denial, and the stranger dashes off into the rain with the blankets, jeering.

The two stand in silence. Then the woodcutter takes the child, saying that he has six and one more will make little difference. The priest thanks him for restoring his faith in man and, as the sky clears, watches him proceed homeward from the steps of the gate.

Not all American critics were favorably impressed with *Rashomon*. Even reviews that praised it contained adjectives such as "slow," "repetitious," "humorlessly solemn," and "confused." The extravagance of the acting was much remarked. Two reviewers, from their mutually distant corners in *Time* and the *New Republic,* singled out the sentimental epilogue as a serious flaw, arbitrarily and unfitly added. It was duly noted that the film draws from the works of the brilliant author Ryunosuke Akutagawa, who committed suicide in 1927 at the age of thirty-five. The basis, however, was not a novel as widely reported, but two short stories. The stories are completely separate, and the scenarist-director, Akira Kurosawa, combined them into a product considerably different from either. The original stories therefore throw some light on the central problem of the film.

The first story, "Yabu no Naka" ["In a Grove"], supplied the basic plot: the conflicting accounts of the same crime by those involved. Akutagawa took an old melodrama and, with the clever detachment for which he is famous, made it ask Pilate's question. The circumstances presented as actual are essentially the same as in the film. Then there are the confessions of the bandit, the wife, and the dead man. That is all. There is no fourth account by an eye witness, no comment on the implications of the testimonies.

The second story, "Rashomon," in addition to the title, contributed the setting, atmosphere, and the idea of characters who discuss right and wrong, duty and necessity. Kyoto has been devastated by a series of natural calamities: earthquakes, whirlwinds, and fires. The Rashomon has fallen into decay and become a hideout for thieves and a depository for unclaimed corpses. A servant of a samurai, just discharged because of hard times, seeks its shelter from the rain. He contemplates the gloomy surroundings and his gloomy prospects, and debates with himself whether or not to become a thief. Climbing the stairs to the tower to find a corner for the night, he comes upon an old woman among the corpses, pulling the hair from one. He seizes her and demands to know what she is doing. She explains that she takes the hair for a wig. The dead woman used to sell snake meat as fish. If she knew the other had to take her hair to live, she probably wouldn't care. Listening, the man makes the decision he could not, earlier. Tearing off the hag's clothes and throwing her down among the corpses, he runs into the night.

Why was an atmosphere of gloom and decay, of physical and spiritual misery, chosen as a background in the film? The original story of the crime contains no such atmosphere, no linking of the event to the conditions of the times. Its effect is all the more striking because of this. If the sole aim of the film was to depict individual lust, selfishness and falsehood as a timeless problem, as favorable American reviews acclaimed, then it could well have been more faithful to the spirit, as well as the words, of Akutagawa in developing the remarkable event in less remarkable circumstances. It should not be forgotten that this film was made in the first instance for Japanese audiences, at a time when Japanese films were only beginning to emerge from an understandable period of complete escapism. A drama laid in medieval Japan, involving questions of human nature, could have provided a respectable type of escape without sacrificing its integrity. Yet the picture opens on the ruined Rashomon: once the great architectural symbol of the capital of Japan, now the crumbling reflection of a devastated city whence the seat of power has moved. It is deluged by a relentless, windless rain. Under the gate sit the priest and the woodcutter, exchanging mute glances and headshakes. The priest slowly recites the kinds of disaster that have befallen. "And now this. I may lose my faith." Later, shrugging off their story, the stranger says, "Who is honest nowadays, anyway?" It is hard to believe that a Japanese audience was not being led to refer to their own experience and to see the events of the story accordingly.

The man and wife are depicted at the outset as the very embodiment of Japanese virtue, refinement, and prosperity. He is a samurai, of the ancient warrior caste whose tradition was so carefully preserved until 1945; handsome, weaponed and well-dressed. As they pass the priest, he turns and laughs happily up at his wife. She is mounted on a fine horse and veiled from view. Lovely and petite, she seemed to the bandit in that first glance, he says, like an angel.

The bandit, as portrayed in the film, is a most remarkable character. In the original story, he wears a blue silk kimono and joins the couple as a traveling companion in order to divert them from the road with talk of buried treasure. There is evidently nothing unusual in his appearance or manner, and he easily disguises his identity and intentions so as to be acceptable. The film Tajomaru, on the other hand, is a half-clad savage, uncouth, insolent, and raucous, who "capers about the screen," as the London *Times* said, "like a ferocious, demented Puck bellowing with maniacal laughter." He appears the least Japanese of all the characters, and a sort of incarnation of the *oni,* or ogre, of Japanese folklore, which has often been interpreted as a representation of the foreigner. His build and movements, even his features, suggest something of the gangling awkwardness that appears in Japanese caricatures of Occidentals. He is alternately terrifying and ridiculous, but always alien to the others. This serves to emphasize the avariciousness and foolishness of the samurai who, significantly, leaves his wife and undertakes the journey to his ruin as a commercial venture.

The scene in which the wife is overcome in a prolonged kiss (in itself still a shocker for Japanese audiences) is more horrifying because her attacker is a sweating, scratching, bug-slapping barbarian than it would have been with Akutagawa's blue-kimonoed outlaw. The strong suggestion of cultural difference, verging on the ethnic, gives her ultimate lustful response an additional meaning. The problem is as old as conquest. And the epilogue of the abandoned child takes on a practical significance which removes from it much of the stigma of artistic error which it must bear if considered only as a disconnected attempt to restore faith in goodness.

In the original story, the wife tells her husband very simply that she cannot live with her disgrace and his contempt, and that she cannot leave him alive as a witness to them. Then she kills him, but fails in her attempt to kill herself. In the film, her confession is, in effect, a plea of temporary insanity. While she does not admit to any guilt in yielding to the bandit, nothing is done to remove the impression made by the scene which shows her to the audience as finally sharing his passion. She sobs hysterically and concludes her story by beseeching the audience—which sits in the position of the judge throughout the testimonies— "But what could I, a poor woman, do?"

The woodcutter, in the original story simply a witness who found the body, becomes an eyewitness whose account provides a devastating contrast to the others. Yet in the end he, too, is implicated, and the truth again eludes the others. Aside from his story, he has a place in the commentary and the epilogue as one of the only two commoners in the picture. The other is a stranger, who accepts human depravity with a laugh, jeers at the struggles of those who would deny it, and makes what he can for himself without scruple. The woodcutter is a simple man, striving to be honest under the burden of a large family and hard times. He is disturbed by a sense of his own guilt and the knowledge of the guilt of the other three. The priest, with less knowledge of the event than the other, shares his feeling with even greater unhappiness, for he perceives its fatal consequences for his faith.

The *Times,* more perspicacious in its perplexity over *Rashomon* than the American accolades, notes that there is little ritual about it and that even the music does not seem to be distinctively Japanese. This touches an important point about the epilogue. The picture has been filled with noise and confusion. Aside from the hysterics of the woman, much of the noise has been the derisive laughter of the bandit and the cynical stranger: the laughter which, even in silence, rings in the ears of a proud man defeated and reduced. There is practically no ritual and all reminders of contemporary Japan are unpleasant. Then, as the woodcutter takes the baby from the priest and goes home, both bow twice, ceremoniously. The priest stands on the steps of the Rashomon, which no longer looks so ruined in the emerging sunlight. The music has suddenly become traditional. The final act of grace has restored a particularly Japanese kind of rightness.

There is a striking similarity with a final scene in *The Well-Digger's Daughter,*[1] where the unmarried mother, the repentant father, and the grandparents, separated by social barriers, are united around the crib of the baby. Raimu, as the well-digger, has a speech in which he urges that the past be forgotten in love for the child. "For here," he says, "is our hope. Here is France." The French in 1946 had need of a hope in which to sink the bitter divisions of the past. Postwar Japan is in need of a belief on which to found a duty. Surely the epilogue of *Rashomon* points, after the unanswerable questions raised in the story, to a basic belief and duty for Japanese to hold to. The old vision of a hopeful future springing from a glorious past is lost, and the way to its recovery lies through a maze of doubtful thoughts about misfortune, guilt, and shame. Yet there is a new Japan, which demands love and care, like the abandoned child, not because of its auspicious or legitimate beginnings, but because it is alive and will perish without them.

It would be foolish to argue that the film is a complete or consistent allegory. To refer again to the *Times* review, however, ". . . something, some hint of a country's habits of thinking, some perhaps unconscious reflection of its prejudices and preferences, filters through the lens of the camera to perplex or amuse the foreigner." Much of the perplexity can be avoided by recognizing the implications for the Japanese audience, intermediate between the basic story and the more universal meaning. These aid the story in supporting the commentary, and fill the picture in spots that would otherwise be empty. They also help to account for the unrestrained, un-Oriental acting. The actors are portraying emotions which Japanese are conditioned by recent events to feel strongly, and their portrayals must be adequate to these feelings as well as to the events of the story. In these terms, even the agonized contortions of the medium as she establishes contact with the spirit of the dead samurai seem to have some meaning.

Rashomon was not popular in Japan on its first showing, although there has been more interest in a second circulation since its international awards. It is not

---

1. Directed by Marcel Pagnol, 1940; re-edited version, 1946.—ED.

a popular-type production, but many circles there have received it enthusiastically. Without substantiating the specific arguments of this review, a prominent Japanese official assured the writer that the significance for the current situation in Japan was widely accepted. Any full understanding of the film, he added, must consider it in terms of the current feelings of Japanese.

The story told by each of the three participants protects his self-respect. In the account of the woodcutter, the common man, they are all revealed as frauds. The fight is a travesty on that described by the bandit, after which the mighty Tajomaru, heaving with fright and exertion, goes off to be betrayed into capture by a rebellion of his own innards. Bitter satire on the heroic virtues finds a natural response in a defeated nation. Still, we are reminded, the woodcutter also has a motive for changing the facts to conceal his guilt.

How did the old beliefs and loyalties die? Did they perish in a defeat at arms which "liberated" those who had already begun to see through them? Did they, in a manner of speaking, annihilate themselves in shame and sorrow for a people no longer worthy of them? Were they destroyed by those who held them dear because they were an unbearable reminder of duties that could no longer be fulfilled? Or were they done in by an uncertain scuffle of ideals and proclamations and conflicting directives that left nothing firm and whole in their place? Finally, since ideals do not die as men die, the question remains, Are they really dead? It seems unlikely that thoughtful Japanese would see *Rashomon* without having some of these questions brought to mind. Even small touches may strike a chord. For example, when the bandit pleads with the woman to go with him and then, impatient at getting no reply, shakes her roughly and shouts, "Say yes, will you!" some might see something of the ambivalent attitude of SCAP.[2]

Just how intentionally Kurosawa worked these overtones into his film is questionable. Since he has taught us so well that the confession of a principal may be a poor guide to truth, perhaps we shall never know. However that may be, he produced an amazing work in *Rashomon* and, despite its roughness, a great motion picture. If the implications for Japanese are those here described, they carry little self-pity and have the same objective balancing of error and guilt into an open question as the rest of the film. This is what makes the solution of the epilogue particularly touching. As an artistic achievement and as a searching of the soul, *Rashomon* is something of which any country could be proud. What it may signify for future developments in Japan, and for relations with the United States, remains to be seen.

---

2. Supreme Commander for the Allied Powers.—ED.

Rashomon

Tadao Sato

In 1950 Akira Kurosawa made two films, *Scandal* and *Rashomon*. The former is a skillfully made small picture which lacks both the thematic strength and the formal beauty of Kurosawa's best work. *Rashomon* is, of course, the picture which made the Japanese art of cinema known in the West after it had won the Grand Prix at the Venice Festival in the following year. More than this, however, the film is among the masterpieces of postwar Japanese cinema. One wants to believe that the West understood this, that its mere exoticism did not win the film the prize. And Alain Robbe-Grillet's remark that *L'Année dernière à Marienbad*[1] was inspired by *Rashomon* would seem to indicate this until one considers the manifold differences between Kurosawa and Robbe-Grillet himself. In Japan the film was admired for its brilliance, and the critics put it among the year's ten-best films, but the general opinion was not inclined to call the film a masterpiece.

Akira Iwasaki has summed up the matter well when he says that "though the disbelief, indeed despair at human nature, the suspicion of objective truth and its reliability, did not win much sympathy from the masses of Japan, it was natural that these thoughts should appeal to West Europe, confronted as it was with a series of real crises."

Yet one wonders if Rashomon indeed represents a disbelief and despair at human nature, a suspicion of objective truth and its reliability. It is difficult to believe that Kurosawa, who has shown the triumph of humanism in such films as *The Quiet Duel, Stray Dog,* and *Scandal,* should suddenly maintain a diametrically opposed opinion—he is simply not the kind of man interested enough in logic to play with its paradoxes. His intentions can be read into what he himself has said of the film. In the final sequence of *Rashomon,* there is the episode where the poor woodcutter takes care of the abandoned baby, resulting in the feeling that, despite what went before, human beings are naturally good. This episode has consequently been much criticized, been called unnatural and sentimental. Kurosawa himself defended it in an interview with Chiyota Shimizu.

Translated by Goro Sato. From *Kurosawa Akira no Sekai* [*The World of Kurosawa*] (Tokyo: Sanichi Shobo, 1968).
1. *Last Year at Marienbad,* screenplay by Robbe-Grillet, directed by Alain Resnais, 1961.—ED.

Shimizu: I think that episode with the baby is wrong—it sounds like a lesson in Christian charity.

Kurosawa: I have a word to say in its excuse. The spirit of our times is suspicious, and I am glad I have no part of it. I simply want people to be happy—though perhaps you may find a kind of escapism in my attitude.

Shimizu: I understand what you mean, but it seems to me that in the film it is all too sudden.

Kurosawa: It's strange—when people talk in a cynical manner, then everyone expresses approval; when someone speaks in an optimistic manner, however, the criticism is general. I question an attitude like that. However, maybe it is, as you say, all too sudden. Maybe I forced this ending on the film—but, on the other hand, I had no other way of ending it.

By which we understand that Kurosawa himself is far from being cynical.

Rashomon is based on a 1921 short story of Ryunosuke Akutagawa, "In a Grove," which in turn was based upon episodes in the tenth-century narrative, *Stories of the Past and Present (Konjaku Monogatari)*. The original narrative is simple. A samurai traveling with his wife is tricked by a bandit who takes them to a grove, ties him up, and rapes the woman. After that the bandit goes away, the warrior and his wife continue their journey, although she blames him for not having prevented this occurrence. Akutagawa made this anecdote into a more complicated story by casting, in the form of seven confessions by the people who were implicated in the rape and murder.

A samurai named Takehiro is said to have been killed by a bandit named Tajomaru; the wife, named Masago, is supposed to have run off. At the police court Tajomaru speaks, as does Masago, and Takehiro himself, through a medium. They and the minor characters all testify and the three principals tell the story from their various viewpoints.

According to Tajomaru, he wanted to leave after raping Masago, but she clung to him, weeping, and saying that either he or her husband had to die. The bandit is proud to state that he won the duel.

According to Masago, after being raped by the bandit, she saw how her husband despised her for what had happened. He told her to kill herself and she, in her distraction, stabbed him.

According to Takehiro—through the medium—Tajomaru, after raping the wife, offered to marry her. She, wanting to go off with him, asked him to kill her husband. Surprised at this, he left her then and there. Therefore he, the husband, killed himself. This is as far as Akutagawa goes.

The story was adapted by Shinobu Hashimoto, a then-unknown writer who had worked with the late Mansaku Itami. Another director, Kiyoshi Saeki, who had also been affiliated with Itami, showed the scenario to Kurosawa and introduced the young writer. From the first, Kurosawa was interested in the work but decided, with Hashimoto's help, to add a fourth confession not in the original—that of a woodcutter. Here the story was that Tajomaru decided to marry Masago and challenged Takehiro to a duel. He, however, protested that such a woman was not worth fighting over. Masago, however, goaded them into a duel, during which she fled.

The episode of the woodcutter sounds as though he is lying, particularly when it comes out that he must himself have stolen the missing murder weapon, the dagger. Yet except for this single point, there was no reason for his lying. After all, the episode of the woodcutter was added not to complicate but to point out that each of the more interested parties had his own reasons for telling the story the way he did—to show himself to be honest.

Actually, *Rashomon* is a work that states a strong belief in the worth of human beings, as well as an equally strong belief in objective truth. Otherwise, there would have been no significance in adding the woodcutter's confession. Although the woodcutter may lie, we are not therefore to draw the conclusion that truth is incomprehensible. Rather, his story shows the humanity of the other three, just as his rescuing the baby at the end shows his own.

Actually, to talk about whether *Rashomon* is humanistic or not is a bit beside the point. If Kurosawa had wanted to prove a humanistic thesis, he probably would not have chosen this material. If he had wanted to prove an antihumanistic thesis he would undoubtedly not have ended the picture as he did. One of the things we know about his intentions is that he was from the first interested in the most cinematic way to tell a story. That he did not think of his film as containing any philosophic or spiritual message is shown by his words upon receiving the Venice prize, when he said that he would have been more gratified if the prize had been given to a film with more contemporary meaning.

Rashomon is a masterpiece because of the way it is made, because of the director's interpretation, his style, his technique. Just how brilliant it is we discover if we compare it to Martin Ritt's *The Outrage,* which is an adaptation of the same scenario and turned out to be so commonplace as not worth the viewing.[2]

One remembers brilliant scenes in the Kurosawa film: the woodcutter (Takashi Shimura) in the grove, the sun shining through the leaves; the wife (Machiko

2. Released in 1964, *The Outrage* starred Paul Newman as the bandit; Laurence Harvey as the husband; Claire Bloom as the wife; Howard da Silva as the "prospector" ("woodcutter" in *Rashomon*); Edward G. Robinson as the "con man" ("commoner" in *Rashomon*); and William

Kyo) assaulted by the bandit (Toshiro Mifune) while her husband (Masayuki Mori) is tied to a tree; when he forcibly kisses her, the sun shines into her eyes, dazzling her. This last is interesting enough to be examined in detail:

161 Long shot. The woman in the foreground, sobbing; Tajomaru in the background. He stalks up to her, she lunges yet again, but now he grabs and holds her. (15 seconds)

162 Medium close-up of the husband watching them; he bows his head. (5 seconds)

163 Close-up. The woman claws Tajomaru's face; he wrests her head free and pushes her to the ground (camera tilts down); she struggles but he kisses her. (7 seconds)

164 The sky (pan) seen through the branches of the trees. (2 seconds)

165 Close-up of the bandit kissing her; she stares straight up. (4 seconds)

166 The sky (pan) seen through overhead branches. (2 seconds)

167 Close-up from reverse angle; Tajomaru holding her, kissing her. (1 second)

168 The sky and trees. The camera no longer pans; the sun shining brilliantly through the branches. (3 seconds)

169 Large close-up from reverse angle: Tajomaru kissing the woman as she stares blankly at the sun. (3 seconds)

170 The sun through the branches; slowly the scene goes out of focus. (4 seconds)

171 Large close-up. The woman closes her eyes. (4 seconds)

172 Large close-up of the dagger in her hand, Tajomaru tightly gripping her wrist. Her fingers loosen, the dagger drops to the ground. (3 seconds)

173 Large close-up of the dagger sticking point first in the ground. (2 seconds)

174 Middle shot of Tajomaru's back, the woman in his arms. The camera slowly dollies toward them. Her hand encircles his back, her fingers move caressingly; she tightens her grip on him: she is giving herself. (11 seconds)

All of this action—and it is merely a bandit kissing a woman—is edited rhythmically, and divided into fourteen different shots, into which are accented over

---

Shatner as the "preacher" ("priest" in *Rashomon*). Based both on Kurosawa's *Rashomon* and on the 1959 Broadway stage adaptation by Fay and Michael Kanin, also called *The Outrage,* the film was directed by Martin Ritt, written by Michael Kanin, and released by Metro-Goldwyn-Mayer.—ED.

and over again the close-ups of the sun. She is herself lost in the dazzle of this sun and the camera moves forward to see the beads of sweat on the bandit's back, glittering under this same sun, as beautiful as diamonds, and in her caressing of this sweat her ecstasy is suggested.

What is lacking in Ritt's *The Outrage* is precisely this exultation, this ecstasy face to face with the sun, this psalm to naked humanity, which gazes at the sun with eyes wide open and feels no regret at exposing itself freely under this sunlight. Extraordinary as this passage is, it does not illustrate the theme of the film. It is followed at once by Takehiro's confession, in which such exultation is made to appear as though it is a crime.

Rashomon is filled with such marvellous images, which once seen are not to be forgotten. There is the sequence where Tajomaru, having tied up Takehiro, runs back shouting to get Masago, the light of the sun dazzling among the leaves; there is in this extremely rhythmically edited sequence—fourteen short shots in all—one of the most brilliant examples of fluent beauty in Japanese cinema.

Here I might mention that I feel that, historically, this kind of passage in Japanese period films is always used in the same kind of situation: in showing us the pathetic beauty of the pursued. This kind of passage has been created by an awareness of the sufferings of someone trying to get away. In these scenes, where the assailant springs upon the prey, Kurosawa is within a known genre but has illuminated it with crystalline beauty. One might indeed find in this passage the meaning of the film. Continuously there are cuts back to the great gate, Rashomon itself, with a heavy rain pouring as though it is trying to wash away the greatest of sins.

And then we must ask the question, What is it then in these desires and exultations that requires mobilization of such sun, such rain? To commit a crime and then to face it, to reach ecstasy itself, looking straight into the sun—such an image has perhaps never before been seen in Japanese cinema. Sin, evil, these belong to the dark night, the melancholy mood—or used to, at any rate. The so-called *taiyo-zoku* (rebellious younger generation) pictures, that came into vogue four years after *Rashomon,* often enough showed the ecstasy of sin under a midsummer sun, yet few of such films in any way paralleled *Rashomon*, except for Kon Ichikawa's 1956 picture, *Punishment Room* (*Shokei no Heya*). What they mostly lacked, despite their casual acceptance of daytime sin, were such things as a continual contrasting downpour, almost washing away the devastated streets of Kyoto, as if to deny an overflowing consciousness of crime.

Here Kurosawa crystallized a genuine style, one that had little to do with faith or lack of it in human beings, but much to do with the exultations and atonements of the individual. The director often uses fierce winds, violent rains, or sunlight enough to give sunstroke. Such are apparently just exaggerated gestures to ensure the effect of dramatic complications, and so they are in his minor works. They are, however, more. Violent wind, rain, light, all have the function of separating a character from his social functions, of confronting him with his own inner reactions. They reflect inner desires or fears, they have nothing to do with a moral consciousness, which is, in itself, social. Not to feel hunted or driven, but to admit desire and self-confidence; not to blame their sins on others but to confess it serenely in the face of the sun and the rain—this is the true pursuit of the genuine self, and it is this that has been so largely lacking in Japanese cinema and could have appeared only now when the moral authority of society was weakened.

Machiko Kyo's most impressive scene is the episode of Masago's confession, in which, after having been violated, she goes to her husband, then sees the scorn in his eyes, and cries, "Don't, don't look at me like that!" She paces back and forth in front of him, near hysteria. The acting of both was most impressive, their best performances in anything. And here, Kurosawa—in a sequence comprising about twenty cuts—cuts back and forth carefully between the characters, who both writhe in separate ways under the feeling of shame, gazing into each other's eyes but each fearing the gaze of the other. These cuts are so adjusted—dollies backward and forward, pans left and right—that the result is a vivid picturization of shame, as though the camera itself were in agony.

Yet the woman, placed in the situation of utmost shame, instead of being conquered by this emotion, finally and boldly stares, putting her full emotional power into this gaze; and the man is stabbed to death and yet continues his gaze of cold contempt—in short, all shameful feelings we see turned into a psalm of life, this clashing together has penetrated and destroyed the emotion of shame by transcending it.

Each of these shots is very short, and their succession gives us the feeling that we are moving along with the camera. She does not want to look at him, yet she must; he, likewise, cannot keep his eyes from her. These shots of them draw their gazes as though a cord existed between the two of them, and us.

Seen in the context of the story, this sequence seems to be portraying only the egoism of the man, the grief of the woman—yet, owing to the acting, to the camera work of Kazuo Miyagawa, the direction of Kurosawa, something far more important results: Only a consciousness of shame can restore beauty to the individual who has lost it. To be conscious of shame is the same as self-respect. For Kurosawa, this point is, I think, the emotional basis for his moral.

The Impact of *Rashomon*
Stanley Kauffmann

W hy should this film have had such a strong impact? Surely not because of the script alone. It is a good enough Pirandellian teaser with somber overtones, but—on paper—it is little more than one more statement of a familiar idea, the contradictory nature of truth, the impossibility of absolutes. On film, because of its cinematic qualities that grow out of the script but surpass .it, *Rashomon* becomes a work of greater size.

One general reason for the film's impact is its cultural accessibility. Many Japanese directors, including at least one who is on Kurosawa's creative plane, Yasujiro Ozu, are more difficult to approach, more "Japanese." Kurosawa has always resisted being labeled a Westerner in any sense that makes him seem unsympathetic to his own culture, but he has always asserted that "the Western and the Japanese live side by side in my mind naturally, without the least sense of conflict." His fine-arts training and his response to Akutagawa, of all Japanese authors, support this thesis. Also, as he has said many times, he greatly admires American directors, especially John Ford, William Wyler, and Frank Capra. So, at Venice in 1951, those who might have expected this film to be couched in the esthetics of Noh or kabuki—which Kurosawa has indeed used elsewhere—found instead a work that was intrinsically Japanese yet certainly not remote in style or dynamics.

But of course there are other values in *Rashomon* that give it stature, much larger and deeper than Kurosawa's cosmopolitanism. Chief among these, I think, are three particular beauties.

First, the acting. As the woodcutter, Takashi Shimura runs through the film like a quiet stream of human concern—human enough to be himself found out in wrongdoing. Shimura, who was trained in the theater, had already played in eight pictures for Kurosawa and later gave (very different) wonderful performances for this director in *The Seven Samurai* and *Ikiru*. The samurai's wife, Machiko Kyo, who began her career as a dancer, is a famous star of Japanese film. The four versions of the murder story provide, in effect, four women to play, each of whom she draws precisely. But the outstanding performance, partly because it is in the most colorful role, is that of Toshiro Mifune as the bandit.

From "Rashomon" in *Living Images* (New York: Harper & Row, 1975).

Mifune, now the best-known Japanese actor in the world, began in films in 1946 after five years in the Japanese army. He made four Kurosawa films before *Rashomon* and made many subsequent ones, including versions of Dostoevsky's *The Idiot,* Shakespeare's *Macbeth,* and Gorki's *The Lower Depths.* He has said of Kurosawa, "I have never as an actor done anything that I am proud of other than with him." Kurosawa has told the story that, while the company was waiting to start on *Rashomon,* they ran off some travelogue films to pass the time, including one about Africa. In it there was a lion roaming around. "I noticed it and told Mifune that that was just what I wanted him to be." Mifune succeeded. He gives one of the most purely feral performances on film—animalistic in both the bestial and the elemental senses, a man concentrated wholly on physical satisfactions and with a fierce power to satisfy them.

The second important aspect of this film is the use of blocks, or plaques, of visual texture. Each of the three main locations of the story has a distinct visual "feel": the gate, the courtyard of the police station where the witnesses testify, and the forest where the stories take place. The gate scenes are drenched in rain. Until the very last moments, each of these gate scenes is seen—and heard— through torrents, frequently emphasized by being shot from ground level so that we see the rain pounding the earth. The fall of the rain is often matched by a vertical view of the scene from above.

In the testimony scenes the witnesses kneel before us, motionless. (We never see the magistrate, who "is" the camera.) In contrast to the gate scenes, these courtyard scenes are sunlit, and the composition is horizontal. Three great parallel bands stretch across the screen: one of shadow, close to us, in which the testifying witnesses kneel; one of sunlight behind it, in which the preceding witnesses kneel; and the top of the low courtyard wall behind them. The camera rarely moves in these scenes. Kurosawa creates a tension between the violent stories being recounted and the serenity of the picture.

The third plaque of texture, the forest, is dappled with sunlight and filled with movement—horizontal as the characters move forward, vertical as the camera frequently looks up at the sun.

These three distinctive textures are, first, aids to our understanding of a complex narrative: we know immediately where we are at every moment. They also provide a contrapuntal texture: the somber setting for the conversation of the troubled woodcutter and the priest and the cynical commoner; the quiet place of recollection; the kinetically lighted and composed setting for the rape and murder.

The last major esthetic component of *Rashomon* is the quality of the motion in those forest scenes. Kurosawa has said:

> I make use of two or three cameras almost all the time. I cut the film freely and splice together the pieces which have caught the action most forcefully, as if flying from one piece to another.

He has made this use of *motion* in motion pictures uniquely his own, and never more "forcefully" than in the forest scenes of *Rashomon*. In the forest, where there is danger to people and, more important, danger to truth, the camera hovers, darts, glides, and swoops, like a skimming bird.

The very opening of the first forest sequence sets the style. Near the end of the gate scene with which the film begins, we are looking down from high above at the men crouched below out of the rain. We cut to a close-up of Shimura's face as he begins to tell his story. Then there is a sharp cut to the bright sun, seen through tree branches as the camera travels forward—a cut accompanied by the sudden entrance of strong rhythmic music. The sequence that follows is dazzling—dazzling both in the virtuosity of the shooting and editing and in the way that these skills are used for mood and point. The next shot is of the woodcutter's axe, on his shoulder, gleaming in the sun as he strides along. Then the camera precedes him as he walks toward us, follows him, and in one especially beautiful moment, arcs across toward him as he strides toward us, crosses in front of him as he approaches, then follows him from the other side. More than underscoring the burst of sunlight and movement into the film, this camera motion sets a tone of comment, of near-teasing, implying, "Stride on, stride on. An ordinary day's work, you think, woodcutter? Stride on. And see." He does see. He and the camera's ballet around him halt suddenly when he spies a woman's hat hanging on a bush. He and the camera resume—and stop again when he spies a man's hat and some other objects. Again he and his observer resume—and this time he halts in horror. We see his face through the upright, death-rigid arms of the slain samurai. The *camera*, fulfilling its implied promise, looks through those arms at the woodcutter's face.

This marvelously intricate and graceful dance of the camera continues through all the versions of the forest story. In a sense we are always aware of it; it would be overly reticent if we were not. The language of a good poem is enjoyable at the same time that the poem moves to something for which the language is only the visible sign. Kurosawa is always sure to make his camera movement, wonderful in itself, inseparable from what it treats. For instance, the bandit and the samurai fight twice, once in the bandit's story, once in the woodcutter's. In the first, both men fence brilliantly. The second fight is a frantic brawl in which both men look foolish. In both encounters the camera leaps around them like an imp, heightening the fever, but the camera rhythms and perspectives match the quality of the fight in each case.

Now since all this camera movement is silken smooth, at the furthest remove from sickening hand-held improvisation, every smallest action of the players and of Kurosawa's camera had to be planned in detail. Tracks had to be built on which the cameras could dolly. These sequences were obviously shot outdoors, in a real forest, so every inch of the camera's traverse had to be prepared, sometimes in a way that allowed a camera to come around and look back—without a break—at the place it had just left, without revealing the tracks on which it had traveled. These technical details of preparation would not be our concern except for what underlies them: a realization of how thoroughly Kurosawa had to know in advance what he was doing and why. A film director does not have the freedom of inspiration, in sequences of this kind, that a theater director or choreographer has. Long-range design is of the essence here; and the quicksilver insight of these designs—their feeling of spontaneous flight—is extraordinary.

That Venice festival audience must have had a bit of a shock when the music began in that first forest scene. Many have noted its strong resemblance to Ravel's *Bolero.* Not by accident. Kurosawa told his composer, Fumio Hayasaka, to "write something like Ravel's *Bolero.*" Apparently the Ravel piece was not then well-known in Japan and had not become something of the self-parody that it now is to Western ears. Western music can be heard in many Kurosawa films. In the films set in the present, it is often used to show the alteration of Japanese culture. Here Kurosawa apparently thought he was appropriating a helpful Western vitality for *Rashomon.* But whatever the effect of that music was or is on Japanese ears, it is still bothersome to ours. Kurosawa is big enough to bear a blemish. If we can forgive Dickens for naming one of his female characters Rosa Bud, we can forgive Kurosawa for his Ravel imitation.

Earlier I noted that *Rashomon,* the film, is a far larger work than its good-enough script. This is a commonplace about any satisfying film, of course, even about some unsatisfying ones, but it has a special pertinence in this case. Kurosawa's vision, his steely yet sympathetic sense of drama, his power to make the screen teem with riches yet without any heavy-breathing lushness, his overwhelming faculties of rhythmic control that translate emotion into motion, all these produce a question in us. We ask: Can such a subtle and complex artist really have bothered to make a film about—as has been said—"the unknowability of truth"? Would that trite theme have been enough for such a man? Finally, the very quality of Kurosawa's art opens up this banal version of relativism to reveal the element that *generates* the relativism: the element of ego, of self. Finally, *Rashomon* deals with the preservaton of self, an idea that—in this film—outlasts earthly life. That idea is not the sanctity of each individual as a political concept, not the value of each soul as a religious concept, but stark, fundamental *amour-propre*. The bandit wants to preserve and defend his ego, the wife hers, and the husband, dead and out of his body, wants the same. Even the woodcutter, who has little *amour-propre* to protect, is forced to tell a more complete version of his story in self-defense.

Ego underlies all, the film says at last. What is good and what is horrible in our lives, in the way we affect other lives, grows from ego: not merely the biological impulse to stay alive but to have that life with some degree of pride.

In the Christian lexicon, pride is the first deadly sin; but in our daily lives, Christian or not, Westerner or Easterner, we know that this sin is at least reliable. We can depend on it for motive power. All of us acknowledge that we ought to be moved primarily by love; all of us know that we are moved primarily by self. *Rashomon* is, essentially, a ruthlessly honest film. Exquisitely made, electrically exciting, it reaches down—by means of these qualities—to a quiet, giant truth nestled in everyone of us. Ultimately what the film leaves with us is candor and consolation: if we can't be saints, at least we can be understandingly human.

The Woman in *Rashomon*

Joan Mellen

Rashomon offers Kurosawa's last fully drawn portrait of a woman. The two Akutagawa stories are set in the era of Lady Murasaki during the end of the Heian period. These tales, upon which the film is based, are by now legendary. A notorious bandit named Tajomaru rapes the wife of a samurai in a forest which is the bandit's hunting ground. The samurai is killed, or dies, and the bandit and the woman are hauled to court to testify in the murder trial. On hand to tell the samurai's side of the story is a medium in touch with the dead man's spirit. A woodcutter has also witnessed the event, and he tells his version to a priest as they sit huddled under the Rashomon Gate, a once impressive structure at the southern entrance to Heian-Kyo (Kyoto) and now, by the twelfth century, fallen into disrepair. Heian Japan is represented, not through the world of Murasaki's amiably promiscuous courtiers, but by the poverty and dissoluton that have permeated the rest of the society. This misery is symbolized by the Rashomon Gate itself, haunted by beggars, thieves and outcasts of one kind or another, a convenient place for people to dump dead bodies at night.

Four versions of the story are told, none of them endorsed by the film and all differing, sometimes in detail and always in essentials. Each of the three principals claims to have killed the samurai. The woodcutter's version has the bandit Tajomaru killing a cowardly samurai screaming for his life at the last moment in a craven whine, the very antithesis of *bushido*[1] and the samurai way. In none of the versions, including her own, is the woman (Machiko Kyo) granted self-respect, dignity, or spiritual value; the samurai (Masayuki Mori), in his own version, fulfills the demands of the warrior code with grace, and Tajomaru (Toshiro Mifune), in all versions, is vital, energetic, and physically magnificent.

Tajomaru's story is told first. Here the woman, Masago, appears as a victim of the fortuitous. As she passes through the forest on horseback, accompanied by her husband on foot, a wind blows her veil aside. Tajomaru, sleeping under a tree, catches a glimpse of her extraordinarily beautiful face. "I thought I saw an angel," he recounts at court. Attempting to rape her, he discovers that she is a

From *The Waves at Genji's Door: Japan Through Its Cinema* (New York: Pantheon Books, 1976).
1. Warrior code.—ED.

demon as well ("she fought like a cat"). It is the feeling Kurosawa wanted Kyo to convey, as, in an oft-repeated anecdote, we are told how he instructed her to imitate the black leopard in a Martin Johnson jungle picture which the cast viewed during the shooting.

Woman is angel outside and demon within, even as, in the culture at large, we are offered the choice of the "good" woman—the faithful wife—or the "bad" woman—the prostitute or whore from whom alone men derive sexual pleasure. Men may not marry the woman of sexual appetite because only absolute monogamy will assure them of reliable heirs, and because frigid, cowed women can be relied upon to accept their lot, no matter what the vagaries of their husband-mates. In the image of Masago in *Rashomon* Kurosawa implicitly expresses the double standard that continues today to define the lives of Japanese women.

As he raped her, the bandit tells us, Masago involuntarily responded. Wife on the outside, she is whore within, a demon more than a woman after all. The camera executes a three-hundred-and-sixty-degree pan of the sky with sun filtering through, in a technique that would only much later become a cliché of sexual response. The dagger Masago had been holding drops, penetrating the earth in a very short take, during which the camera does not focus on the weapon so that the sexual symbolism will not be overstated. Masago grips Tajomaru tightly and her eyes close. A few moments later she will insist that one of the men must die or she will feel "doubly disgraced." She must "belong" to the stronger. But after Tajomaru kills her husband, he, in his account, has her lose her nerve and run away. Looking back upon the experience with a philosophical eye, Tajomaru concludes, "About that woman—it was her temper that interested me, but she turned out to be just like any other woman." There is no one present to say otherwise.

It may be argued that this is how the woman was seen by a lustful bandit who could not possibly do justice to the character of his victim. All versions agree that the rape occurred. But lest we, doubting Tajomaru, are encouraged to value Masago too highly, Kurosawa follows with her account of the events. She emerges in her own testimony as pathetic. She tells us that after the rape (which she is too modest to describe), she wept before the scornful look of her husband and buried her face in the ground. Unable to bear his scorn, she begged him to kill her. Receiving no response, she killed him instead, fainted, and, upon waking, fled. At the trial she plays on the sympathies of the judge we never see, crying and pleading: "I tried to kill myself. But, I failed. What could a poor helpless woman like me do?" When all else fails, she sinks to the ground. Hearing about this from the woodcutter, a commoner huddled for warmth under the Gate doubts her immediately: "Women lead you on with their tears; they even fool themselves." Cynic though he is, his assessment of Masago's performance is too accurate for us to doubt that at this moment the commoner, as an "Every-man," speaks for the director.

Masago figures least in the version told by her dead husband, as if her exis-tence had never been of much account to him. He tells us that she responded with radiance to the bandit's lovemaking and he had never in all their life together "seen her more beautiful." She begged Tajomaru to take her with him, but first to kill her husband. He refused because the worst man is better in character than the best woman, social class notwithstanding. It is a graphic example of why, in Japan, the liberation of women will necessitate a restructuring of the entire so-ciety. The husband, in keeping with the code of honor by which he had always lived in good faith, performs his own *seppuku*.[2]

In the final story, that of the woodcutter, the woman is the most demonic. Laughing hysterically at her predicament, she calls both men fools, attacking their manhood in order to extricate herself from a situation in which she has lost all honor. She has accepted their judgment of her, internalized it, and now flaunts her baseness. Yet the men are reluctant to fight for her, another implication of the sense of true male supremacy which suffuses this film. To provoke the fight, she must spit on Tajomaru. And he, although a bandit and a murderer, is made the better human being by Kurosawa. He is allowed to forgive her; even the wood-cutter feels a form of kinship with this ruthless bandit against the woman. "Women cannot help crying, they are naturally weak," says Tajomaru in the woodcutter's story.

In *Rashomon* woman is perceived as castrating female taunting competing males for not being "real men." "A woman can be won only by strength, by the strength of the swords you are wearing," she screeches near the end of the film. And it is with this view of her character that Kurosawa leaves us. He has given no grounds for belief in Masago's own story, the only one in which she does not respond passionately to the bandit. And even in that story, she is a murderess. Her punishment is presented implicitly as a just reward for her having assumed the role of docile wife under blatantly false pretenses.

After *Rashomon*, Kurosawa seemed to have abandoned his interest in the po-tential of women, as if repelled by Masago, that half-demon of his own creation.

---

2. Hara-Kiri.—Ed.

His response is parallel to that of the culture itself. Women are rendered power-less and subordinate and hence reduced, like Masago, to manipulation or deceit for influence and survival. Then the image of the feline woman is reified by male perpetrators into a stereotype. It is a classic example of the self-fulfilling proph-ecy and the prototype of all social victimization, unmediated in the Japanese film by the presence of women directors, with the exception of a few minor directorial efforts by the actress Kinuyo Tanaka. And once, of course, the stereotype is elevated to a symbol in the arts, presented as an image of truth, the impact of this perpetuated myth in turn conditions the view women have of themselves. It is indeed a vicious circle, as yet unbroken in Japan by profound social change.

The Dialectic of Light and Darkness in Kurosawa's *Rashomon*

Keiko I. McDonald

Akira Kurosawa's *Rashomon,* the winner of both the 1951 Venice Festival Grand Prize and the 1952 Academy Award for Best Foreign Film, has been examined from many perspectives. One Japanese critic has pointed to the non-Japanese qualities of *Rashomon* and Kurosawa's other major films, and another critic has commented on its fine filmic style. A number of Western critics have explored the moral, psychological, and social implications of the murder in the film and its consequence. When he was once asked what *Rashomon* is about, Kurosawa simply stated that the film is about rape and nothing more. This statement by Kurosawa encourages us to interpret the film in any possible way that will satisfy our critical propensity. No critic has yet approached *Rashomon* from the vantage point of symbolism, even though this perspective offers a key insight into the central problem of this difficult film: "What is man's nature?"

Rashomon is pervaded by a dialectic of symbols of light and darkness. The murder takes place in a dense, dark forest. The main actions of the priest, the woodcutter, and the commoner are set against the pouring rain. The half-ruined gate standing in the torrent gives the film a gloomy setting. In sharp contrast to these dark images are impressionistically filmed images of sunlight. The blazing sun piercing the clouds dominates the police station. Sunlight coming through the trees flickers on the woodcutter's ax. When the wife yields to the bandit, she looks up at the sun glittering through the branches. At the conclusion of the film the woodcutter walks into the sunlight after the rainstorm is over. The juxtaposition of these symbols serves as an important, basic constituent, which contributes to a unified version of the film.

Rashomon opens with ten rapid shots of a half-ruined gate, the Rashomon, in the midst of a downpour. These shots are followed by the subtitle, which reads: "Kyoto, in the twelfth century when famines and civil wars had devastated the ancient capital." In the following scene the gloom these natural and man-made

From *Cinema East* (Madison, N.J.: Fairleigh Dickinson University Press, 1983).

calamities connote is intensified by the priest's remark: "Wars, earthquakes, great winds, fires, famines, plague—each new year is full of disaster." So it was in the twelfth century, which marked Japan's transition from aristocracy to feudalism; it was a period characterized by political turmoil. Buddhist religious thinkers of that century believed that they were witnessing the final degenerate phase of the world, which would soon end in apocalypse. Disasters like those mentioned by the priest were taken as signs of the world's approaching end.

It is thus clear why the movie starts with a keen awareness of the fragmented state of the world. Both the ruined state of the Rashomon gate, once the splendid southern entrance to the capital, and the violent rain symbolize the chaos prevailing in the world. Yet, two major components of the gate—the gargoyle and the signboard—appear intact amid the devastation. The integrity of these two religious symbols implies that religion has not been completely destroyed but, in fact, holds out a potential for the restoration of order.

Immediately after the second close-up of the signboard, which bears the characters, "Rashomon," the woodcutter begins to recount his discovery of the murdered samurai. A flashback swiftly takes the viewer to the forest where the murder took place. When the woodcutter's story ends, the dark forest suddenly yields to the sunlit police station where the priest, the woodcutter, the wife, and the thief are brought out. First, the priest offers his version of what happened. Then the thief, Tajomaru, provides his version of the story, which we are shown taking place in the forest. When the thief finishes his story, the forest suddenly vanishes as we return first to the police station, and then swiftly again to the half-ruined Rashomon gate. This same pattern of transitions is repeated as the wife tells her version of the story, and the husband his. The tight architectonics of the flashback is important for three reasons. First, each time the scene is cut back to the gate where the film started, the debate over man's nature between the priest and the commoner becomes more intense. Second, the flashback molds Kurosawa's basic design of the dual symbolism: from the darkness of the forest to the light of the police station and back again to the darkness in the gate. Third, the three repetitive geographical changes make a smooth transition to the woodcutter's nature that has occupied the priest and the commoner.

When Tajomaru has explained how the rape took place, the commoner, the woodcutter, and the priest start discussing the reliability of his testimony. The woodcutter simply states that Tajomaru's confession is "a lie." By so doing, the woodcutter functions as an instigator increasing the intensity of argument between the priest and the commoner, who explain their own reasons for rejecting

Tajomaru's version. Both the commoner and the priest agree that man is by nature a liar. However, this very agreement reveals their radically different perspectives on human nature. The commoner is realistic; he assumes that man is innately an impulsive and selfish creature. He further claims that it is thus impossible to avoid lies, especially in difficult times like the present. On the other hand, the priest is idealistic; he assumes that man is basically a rational creature. He argues that deception is a part of an illusion that man cultivates as a necessary tool in confronting the hostile reality of life. The two scenes at the gate, which respectively follow the woman's and the husband's (through the medium's mouth) narrations, clarify these two antithetical perspectives on man's nature. In response to the woodcutter's insistence that their stories are equally untruthful, the priest says: "I must not believe that men are so sinful." Conversely, the commoner says: "After all, who's honest nowadays? Look, everyone wants to forget unpleasant things, so they make up stories."

From this discussion, the central problem of the film is evident: "Is man's nature essentially rational or impulsive, good or bad?" The film presents three basic answers in response. A rationalistic answer is presented by the priest, a primitivistic answer is represented by the commoner, and a melioristic response emerges in the final part of the film. This final answer, given through the woodcutter, is a synthesis of the previous two stances. It claims that man's character includes a separation between reason and impulse, but that man is good to the extent that he tries to reduce this separation. From this perspective, the different versions of the murder in the forest can be taken all together as an answer to the central problem. Kurosawa seems to say we must probe the question of man's nature by playing the various accounts of the murder against one another. The existence of the conflicting stories implies that if man is put through the ordeal of life, the way he acts will reveal his inner nature.

This philosophic concern with man's inner nature as revealed through his behavior is also a feature of Kurosawa's samurai films, such as *The Throne of Blood* and *Seven Samurai*. In *The Throne of Blood,* Washizu, the Japanese Macbeth, swept by his "bolting ambition" into the turmoil of civil war, is trapped in an intellectual maze that causes his destruction. The seven samurai are initially motivated by a desire to satisfy their hunger and agree to help the seemingly hopeless farmers; however, through their battles with bandits, the samurai gradually become altruists. It is not their words but their actions that illuminate the samurai's inner nature. The theme of the revelaton of man's inner reality is also explored in such naturalistic novels as Joseph Conrad's *Heart of Darkness,* which evolves around a man's metaphysical journey into the depths of his heart. These films and literary works present man as a combination of an outer self and an inner self: the outer self, donning a social mask, is controlled by reason that affiliates itself with existing ethical norms; on the other hand, the inner self is controlled by impulses.

The implications of light and darkness are rather opaque in *Rashomon*. On one level, the dichotomy of light and darkness, then, can be considered as an archetypical representation of this bifurcation of man's nature: light represents reason whereas darkness represents impulse. Significantly, darkness is treated as negative until the final sequence of the film because Kurosawa presents impulses as deviations from man's moral consciousness. Then, at the second level, light represents good in man whereas darkness represents evil.

When the woodcutter goes into the dark woods at the beginning of *Rashomon*, the sun is flickering on his ax through the bushes. This glinting sun, which most critics cite as a prime example of Kurosawa's impressionism, symbolizes the exertion of man's moral consciousness over his impulsive action. As the woodcutter continues on into the forest, the sky is again visible through the branches of the trees overhead. The repeated juxtaposition of light and darkness keeps reminding the viewer of the bifurcation of man's nature. The woodcutter first finds a woman's hat with a veil on a branch of a tree. Then he finds a man's hat at his feet, and then a piece of rope. Finally he comes upon an amulet case lying on the leaves. Kurosawa films these objects all in close-up, calling our attention to their symbolic significance. The hats are important social symbols of the station of the samurai and his wife. The amulet case represents man's adherence to religion. Combined with the sense of liberation implied by the torn rope, the abandoned social adornments symbolize the elimination of layers of the social mask, hence, the outer self.

Thus, what happened to the woodcutter, the samurai, his wife, and the thief in the forest is, on a symbolic level, a centripetal regression into the inner self. The apparently incongruous stories given by these four, however, lead us to believe that each person's self-image is radically different from the image he conveys to the others. The woodcutter confesses that he has not seen the dagger that penetrated the husband's chest, and therefore, he is innocent of its theft. The commoner claims, however, that there is good reason to believe that the woodcutter stole the dagger. Although the wife, Masago, insists that she was raped, the stories given by her husband and Tajomaru affirm that she enjoyed the sexual encounter. The woodcutter's story and Masago's describe the husband as lacking in physical strength and being devoid of compassion. On the contrary, the husband's version asserts that he was true to the samurai code. In his confession, Tajomaru stresses his bravery and skill at swordsmanship. However, in the woodcutter's story, the duel between Tajomaru and the samurai, in which they "crossed swords over twenty times" is the very antithesis of the ideal samurai duel. Tajomaru is described as an equal match only because the samurai is a weak, poor swordsman.

Assimilating the stories related by these four characters, we can make a reasonable deduction that each character succumbed to his inner nature in a precarious situation. The woodcutter, a victim of his greed, loses the power to curb his urge to steal the dagger. The film's visual action presents the woodcutter flabbergasted, dropping his glittering ax upon encountering the samurai's corpse. This gesture externalizes his loss of control.

Likewise, Masago yielded to passion though initially reason tried to suppress her impulse. Kurosawa elaborately cinematizes her moral dilemma through the juxtaposition of light and darkness. When the bandit starts kissing her, she looks straight up into the sunlight. The swift crosscutting between Masago staring up into the sun and the dazzling sunlight penetrating the branches culminates in a slow fade-out of the sun. The fade-out is immediately succeeded by a close-up of Masago closing her eyes—a gesture emblematic of her loss of reason. As she lets go of her outer nature, Masago lets go of her dagger, the means of protection that a samurai's wife characteristically carried. The camera slowly tracks up toward Tajomaru and Masago, and catches her fingers in a medium shot as her grip on Tajomaru becomes gradually tighter.

In the depths of the forest, the samurai has disclosed his fear, cowardice, and selfishness, completely contrary to his outwardly stern *bushido*[1] nature. As described by the woodcutter, when the samurai frees himself from the rope, he tells Tajomaru, nervously retreating from the bandit: "Stop! I refuse to risk my life for such a woman." Rather than protecting his wife from the bandit, the samurai tries to protect himself. When the samurai and the bandit eventually do start to fight after Masago's provocative remarks that both of them should prove themselves to be real men by fighting, the samurai's action betrays his weakness and ineptitude. Kurosawa's camera work helps to visualize the samurai's cowardice. By persistently employing a medium shot deploying both the samurai and Tajomaru along an almost horizontal line, Kurosawa emphasizes not only the

1. Warrior's code.—ED.

samurai's consciousness of Tajomaru as an equal match but also his timorousness. Another device used by Kurosawa is the frequent presentation of the samurai's physiognomy in a medium shot. This is an effective device for drawing our attention to the samurai's emotion even as it keeps us from becoming too much involved in it. For example, when the samurai slowly advances toward Tajomaru, the medium shot of the samurai's face reveals terror. Consequently, as we expected, he fails to meet the opponent's challenge as a samurai and screams: "I don't want to die! I don't want to die!"

More surprisingly, Tajomaru, whom the commoner describes as "worse than all the other bandits in Kyoto" has yielded to cowardice in the forest. During the battle, as narrated by the woodcutter, Kurosawa pervasively resorts to a medium shot of Tajomaru's face full of his fear and anxiety. Kurosawa also takes care in the visual alignment of Tajomaru and the samurai. In Tajomaru's own story, Kurosawa lets the bandit's back dominate the screen while placing the samurai at the further end. Conversely, in the woodcutter's version, a medium shot of Tajomaru and the samurai aligned on a horizontal line across the screen forms the basic composition. This ironic contrast plays down the bandit's powerfulness and conveys to us the emptiness of his bravado. Consequently, when the samurai advances, Tajomaru's arms start shaking violently. Tajomaru approaches the samurai slowly and fearfully. Finally, when Masago runs into the woods, Tajomaru collapses on the ground.

Exposed to the sunlight at the police station, the woodcutter, the samurai, Masago, and Tajomaru all tell their stories, faithful to their own illusions of what they should be. The sunlight over their heads symbolizes their return to reason. They don their social masks and confess in a manner that will protect their self-images and justify their actions. In contrast to the earlier scenes of the forest, the police station scene is dominated by Kurosawa's more restrictive camera movement and visual composition. The priest, the woodcutter, the wife, and the bandit all sit in a line across the screen, and they are shot from the eye level of the policeman taking their testimony. The camera angle elevates us to the position of the police, the objective judge. The fact that each person is avoiding the eyes of the camera as if afraid of the judgment encourages us to search below the surface in order to distinguish reality from appearance. Interestingly, in the forest scenes Kurosawa pervasively used the point-of-view shot to emphasize each narrator's view of the others involved in the murder. However, the shift in his camera work does not necessarily correspond to the shift in our perspective from identification to detachment. Rather, this change in the camera work augments our sense of detachment, i.e., outside view, which is necessary for a coherent reading of the film.

At this stage the conflicting narrations may yield a tentative acceptance of the commoner's view of man's nature; man is an impulsive creature when confronted with the fragmented world. However, the final interaction of the woodcutter, the priest, and the commoner not only clarifies the three views of man's nature more fully but also asserts the stance represented by the woodcutter. When the wood-cutter's second story finally ends the series of stories, Kurosawa brings us back to the Rashomon gate, to the realist and idealist, the commoner and the priest. It is still raining. The commoner says: "The world we live in is a hell." None of the testimony has moved him an inch from his "realistic" view of human existence as a matter of dog-eat-dog. Significantly the commoner's attire itself sym-bolically affirms his stance. At the beginning of the film, he takes off his shirt and is filmed half-naked, that is, without his social mask.

Similarly, the priest reasserts his idealistic view that man is capable of good; that even when man lies, he lies through recourse to reason, even if it is a purely selfish reason like self-defense. The priest prefers rational moral bad choices to chaotic impulsive violence. The priest's decent robes symbolically correspond to the stance that man assumes many layers of social disguise.

With the introduction of the image of the baby, the film's action takes a radical turn. It moves from the static to the dynamic. Turning away from their debate over man's nature, the priest, the commoner, and the woodcutter now act out their respective views. The subsequent scenes mark the beginning of the final answer to the hitherto sustained central problem. When the commoner sees the baby, his reaction is to kneel over it and strip it of its clothes. The commoner acts out his view that man is impulsive. At the same time his action is presented as negative because the baby is a symbol of fertility and future, and the theft of its clothes constitutes the extermination of hope for a better society. On the other hand, both the priest and the woodcutter respond to the situation rationally. They rush to-ward the baby, whom the priest holds protectively. The woodcutter, who has been verbally inexpressive of his own view of man's nature, now shows his opinion through action; he tries to support the priest's view and defend goodness, which he thinks still remains within man. The woodcutter accuses the commoner of being evil and selfish, and calls his conduct atrocious.

Earlier Kurosawa introduced the abandoned amulet case, but this time he in-troduces an amulet case fastened to the baby. This amulet case makes us aware of the possibility of future religious salvation in this fragmented world. In response to the woodcutter's accusation, the commoner says: "And what's wrong with it? That's the way we are, the way we live. Look, half of us envy the lives that dogs lead. You just can't live unless you're what you call selfish."

The subsequent cinematic action portrays a struggle between the woodcutter and the commoner in the rain. The scene is symbolically crucial in that it externalizes the tension between the primitivism asserted by the commoner and the rationalism asserted by the priest and now tentatively assumed by the woodcutter. The destructive rain, in which the battle is set, symbolizes the social milieu that places these two metaphysical positions in conflict. Their battle ends when the commoner accuses the woodcutter of stealing the dagger. The woodcutter says: "All men are selfish and dishonest." Yet, unlike the commoner, the woodcutter tries to justify man's inclination toward primitivism on the ground of social determinism. He says: "They all have excuses, the bandit, the husband . . ." Deeply affected by the commoner's statement that he "may have fooled the police," the woodcutter's conviction that man is rational and good has now become totally shaken.

In order to dramatize the ascendancy of primitivism over rationalism, which ensues from the conflict between the woodcutter and the commoner, Kurosawa plays upon contrasting physiognomy: the commoner's triumphant, smiling face and the woodcutter's sad, guilty face, both taken in close-up. The commoner continues to push the woodcutter toward the priest, who has been watching the struggle between the two. The commoner's accusation continues: "And so where is that dagger? Did the earth open up and swallow it? Or did someone steal it? Am I right? It would seem so. Now there is a really selfish action for you." Kurosawa swiftly cuts from a medium shot of the commoner slapping the woodcutter to a close-up of the priest holding the baby.

The following long shot, which is focused on the three men under the half-ruined gate, once again imposes a distancing effect upon us, and encourages us to contemplate the three possible views of man's nature. The commoner disappears into the rain, leaving the other two under the gate. By associating the commoner with the torrent, Kurosawa seems to equate the primitive with the destructive side of man's nature and thus to discourage us from accepting this view. The next long shot shows the half-ruined gate, looming above the two men who seem extremely small, intensifying the sense of man's hopelessness in coping with environmental forces.

The three shots following the commoner's disappearance into the rain are thematically significant in three respects. First, these shots, each terminated by a dissolve, mark a radical transition from darkness to light. Second, the dialectic of the two perspectives on man's nature now assumed by the woodcutter and the priest is kept in a tension that will later yield to resolution. A long shot of the priest and the commoner standing under the gate is quickly taken over by a medium shot of both men. At precisely this moment the sound of the rain ceases. Another medium shot of the two remains to be presented while the raindrops thin. Next, a close-up of the priest and the woodcutter under the gate is projected, and the silence is suddenly broken by the baby's cry. The rhetorical stance imposed upon the audience is detachment, since the succession of the simultaneous shots of these two men keeps the audience from identifying with either of them. Again Kurosawa visualizes the polar views through physiognomy; whereas the priest's face is almost impassive, the woodcutter's face is full of remorse, guilt, and compassion.

Referring to the dissolve, which terminates each of the three shots, Donald Richie states that this technique usually means time passing, that it is at the same time a formal gesture, "a gesture which makes us look, makes us feel. Thus, the final important function of the three shots is that the dissolve emphasizes the lapse of psychological time during which the woodcutter's mind goes through a radical transformation—a transformation which might have escaped the audience's attention had a simple cut been used. The guilt and remorse over what the woodcutter did in the forest awaken compassion for the foundling. Precisely at this juncture, reason and impulse join in harmony in his mind. Compassion, a most important Buddhist principle, becomes the root of his moral consciousness: it is what society would have him act upon. The transition from rain into sunlight clearly corresponds to the woodcutter's psychological change.

The following scene reveals that the priest's hitherto unshaken assumption that man is rational and benign has been somewhat affected by what he has thus far witnessed. When the woodcutter tries to take the baby, the priest recoils. The woodcutter humbly responds: "I have six children of my own. One more wouldn't make it any more difficult." The priest apologizes for having suspected the woodcutter's motive: "No. I'm grateful to you. Because, thanks to you, I think I will be able to keep my faith in men."

After the finale of traditional Japanese music, the woodcutter leaves the gate into the sunlight, with the infant in his arms. It is clear, from what we have observed, that the symbolic transition from darkness to light signifies that altruism offers a potential for harmony even in the fragmented world of *Rashomon*. At the same time this transition signifies that man's nature is melioristic as found in the woodcutter's behavior.

However, the last two shots significantly modify this critical deduction. First,

Kurosawa presents a long shot from behind the woodcutter as he walks into the sunlight in vivid contrast to the shadow over the gate. Then the camera swiftly moves to a long shot of the woodcutter from the opposite angle. As he walks toward the camera, he stops and bows to the priest, beaming with happiness. However, despite the woodcutter's magnificent display of optimism, we are visually deluded, for now we are given the impression that the woodcutter is walking into the shadow while the whole gate and the clear sky come into frame behind him.

This reversal of the light and darkness, the shadow and sunlight, which has hitherto been neglected by Kurosawa's critics, seems to deny the optimistic tone with which most viewers see the film end. Rather, it stresses the difficulty of maintaining a melioristic stance in the fragmented world. Concerning the ending of *Rashomon,* Kurosawa himself says that he wanted to present gigantic columns of clouds (cumulo nimbus) above the gate, but they never appeared during the shooting of the final scene. The image of cumulo nimbus predicting approaching rain, though an external datum, serves as another justification for supporting the relativity of man's nature as the film's final implication.

Filmography and Bibliography

Kurosawa Filmography, 1943–1985

The list that follows cites the script writer and script source for all of Kurosawa's films that have been released. A complete filmography may be found in *The Films of Akira Kurosawa* by Donald Richie, Revised Edition (see Bibliography).

1943 *Sanshiro Sugata*
Screenplay by Akira Kurosawa, based on the novel *Sanshiro Sugata* by Tsuneo Tomita (Tokyo: Kinjo Shuppon Sha, 1942).

1944 *The Most Beautiful (Ichiban Utsukushiku)*
Screenplay and scenario by Akira Kurosawa.

1945 *Sanshiro Sugata Part Two (Zoku Sanshiro Sugata)*
Screenplay and scenario by Akira Kurosawa, based on the novel *Sanshiro Sugata, Part Two* by Tsuneo Tomita (Tokyo: Kinjo Shuppon Sha, 1944).

1945 *The Men Who Tread on the Tiger's Tail (Tora No O o Fumu Otokotachi)*
Screenplay and scenario by Akira Kurosawa, based on the Kabuki drama *Kanjincho*. English translation by A. C. Scott (Tokyo: Hokuseido Press, 1963).

1946 *Those Who Make Tomorrow (Asu O Tsukuru Hitobito)*
Scenario by Yusaku Yamagata and Kajiro Yamamoto.

1946 *No Regrets for Our Youth (Waga Seishun Ni Kuinashi)*
Scenario by Eijiro Hisaita and Akira Kurosawa.

1947 *One Wonderful Sunday (Subarashiki Nichiyobi)*
Scenario by Keinosuke Uegusa and Akira Kurosawa.

1948 *Drunken Angel (Yoidore Tenshi)*
Scenario by Keinosuke Uegusa and Akira Kurosawa.

1949 *The Quiet Duel (Shizukanaru Ketto)*
Screenplay and scenario by Senkichi Taniguchi and Akira Kurosawa, based on the play *Shizukanaru Ketto* by Kazuo Kikuta.

1949 *Stray Dog (Nora Inu)*
Scenario by Ryuzo Kikushima and Akira Kurosawa.

1950 *Scandal (Shubun)*
Scenario by Ryuzo Kikushima and Akira Kurosawa.

1950 *Rashomon*
Screenplay and scenario by Shinobu Hashimoto and Akira Kurosawa, based on two stories by Ryunosuke Akutagawa: "Rashomon" and "In a Grove." English publication: *Rashomon and Other Stories,* trans. Takashi Kojima (New York: Liveright Publishing Corp., 1952).

1951 *The Idiot (Hakuchi)*
Screenplay and scenario by Eijiro Hisaita and Akira Kurosawa, based on Feodor Dostoyevsky's novel *The Idiot.*

1952 *Ikiru*
Scenario by Shinobu Hashimoto, Hideo Oguni, and Akira Kurosawa.

1954 *Seven Samurai (Shichinin No Samurai)*
Scenario by Shinobu Hashimoto, Hideo Oguni, and Akira Kurosawa.

1955 *Record of a Living Being/I Live in Fear (Ikonomo No Kiroku)*
Scenario by Shinobu Hashimoto, Hideo Oguni, and Akira Kurosawa.

1957 *The Throne of Blood (Kumonosu-Jo)*
Screenplay and scenario by Shinobu Hashimoto, Ryuzo Kikushima, Hideo Oguni, and Akira Kurosawa, based on William Shakespeare's play *Macbeth.*

1957 *The Lower Depths (Donzoko)*
Screenplay and scenario by Hideo Oguni and Akira Kurosawa, based on Maxim Gorky's play *The Lower Depths.*

1958 The Hidden Fortress (Kakushi Torida No San-Akunin)
Scenario by Shinobu Hashimoto, Ryuzo Kikushima, Hideo Oguni, and Akira Kurosawa.

1960 *The Bad Sleep Well (Warui Yatsu Hodo Yoku Nemuru)*
Scenario by Shinobu Hashimoto, Hideo Oguni, Ryuzo Kikushima, Eijiro Hisaita, and Akira Kurosawa.

1960 *Yojimbo*
Scenario by Ryuzo Kikushima and
Akira Kurosawa.

1962 *Sanjuro*
Screenplay and scenario by Ryuzo
Kikushima, Hideo Oguni, and Akira
Kurosawa, based on the novel *Tsubaki
Sanjuro* by Shugoro Yamamoto.

1963 *High and Low (Tengoku To
Jigoku)*
Screenplay and scenario by Ryuzo
Kikushima, Hideo Oguni, and Akira
Kurosawa, based on the novel *King's
Ransom* by Ed McBain (New York:
Simon & Schuster, 1959).

1965 *Red Beard (Akahige)*
Screenplay and scenario by Ryuzo
Kikushima, Hideo Oguni, Masato
Ide, and Akira Kurosawa, based
on the novel *Akahige* by Shugoro
Yamamoto (Tokyo: Bungei Shunju
Shin Sha, 1959).

1970 *Dodeskaden (Dodesukaden)*
Screenplay by Hideo Oguni, Shinobu
Hashimoto, and Akira Kurosawa,
based on the novel *Shiki Ga Nai
Machi* by Shugoro Yamamoto (Tokyo:
Bungei Shunju Shin Sha, 1962).

1975 *Dersu Uzala*
Scenario by Akira Kurosawa and
Yuri Nagibin, based on *Dersu, the
Trapper* by Vladimir Arseniev, trans.
Malcolm Burr (London: Secker &
Warburg, 1939).

1980 *Kagemusha*
Scenario by Akira Kurosawa and
Masato Ide.

1985 *Ran*
Scenario by Hideo Oguni, Masato
Ide, and Akira Kurosawa, based
on William Shakespeare's play,
King Lear.

Selected
Bibliography

The most complete Kurosawa bibliography in English has been compiled by Patricia Erens in *Akira Kurosawa: A Guide to References and Resources;* see also the bibliography in Donald Richie, *The Films of Akira Kurosawa,* Revised Edition. Many reviews and critical essays are reprinted by Donald Richie in *Focus on Rashomon.* (See below for full references to these volumes.)

Part One of this limited bibliography lists both shorter pieces on *Rashomon* not reprinted in this volume or in *Focus on Rashomon* and works on Kurosawa and on Japanese film which are of major interest beyond their specific treatment of this film. Part Two lists the previously published scripts of Kurosawa's films.

Part One

Anderson, Joseph L. and Donald Richie. *The Japanese Cinema: Art and Industry.* Expanded Edition. Princeton: Princeton University Press, 1982: 223–225.

Bock, Audie E. *Japanese Film Directors.* Tokyo: Kodansha International, 1978: 170–174.

Burch, Noël. *To the Distant Observer: Form and Meaning in the Japanese Cinema.* Berkeley: University of California Press, 1979: 296–298.

Erens, Patricia, ed. *Akira Kurosawa: A Guide to References and Resources.* Boston: G. K. Hall, 1979.

Giuglaris, Shinobu and Marcel Giuglaris. *Le Cinéma japonais.* Paris: Editions du Cerf, 1956.

Japan Film Center. *Kurosawa: A Retrospective* [program booklet]. New York: Japan Society, 1981: 48–49.

Kauffmann, Stanley. *"Rashomon."* In *Living Images*. New York: Harper and Row, 1975: 316–324.

Kurosawa, Akira. *Something Like an Autobiography*. Trans. Audie E. Bock. New York: Alfred A. Knopf, 1982: 180–189.

Leyda, Jay. "The Films of Kurosawa." *Sight and Sound* (October/December, 1954): 74–78.

Linden, George W. "Five Views of *Rashomon.*" *Soundings* (Winter, 1973): 393–411.

Mellen, Joan. *The Waves at Genji's Door: Japan through Its Cinema*. New York: Pantheon, 1976: 46–50.

Rayns, Tony. "Tokyo Stories" [interview with Kurosawa]. *Sight and Sound* (Summer, 1981): 170–174.

Richie, Donald. "Akira Kurosawa." *Orient-West* (Tokyo) (Summer, 1962): 45–55.

———. "Dostoevsky with a Japanese Camera." *Horizon* (July, 1962): 42–47. Reprinted in Lewis Jacobs, ed., *The Emergence of Film Art*. New York: Hopkinson and Blake, 1969: 330–337.

———. *The Films of Akira Kurosawa*. Berkeley: University of California Press, 1965: 70–80. Revised Edition, 1984: 70–80.

———, ed. *Focus on Rashomon*. Englewood Cliffs, N.J.: Prentice-Hall, 1972

———. *Japanese Cinema: Film Style and National Character*. Garden City, N.Y.: Doubleday, 1971: 227–231.

———. *The Japanese Movie*. Tokyo: Kodansha International, 1966: 91. Revised Edition, 1982.

———. "Kurosawa on Kurosawa" [interview]. *Sight and Sound* (Summer, 1964): 108–113; (Autumn, 1964): 200–203.

———. "Rashomon." *Encyclopedia of Japan, VI*. Tokyo: Kodansha International, 1983: 283–284.

Sadoul, Georges. "Existe-t-il un néo-realisme japonais?" *Cahiers du Cinéma* (November, 1953): 7–19.

Sato, Tadao. *Currents in Japanese Cinema*. Trans. Gregory Barrett. Tokyo: Kodansha International, 1982: 15–30.

Tucker, Richard N. *Japan: Film Image*. London: Studio Vista, 1973: 74–84.

Part Two

A bilingual edition of *The Complete Works of Akira Kurosawa* was projected by Kinema Jumpo-Sha, Tokyo, 1970–1971, with English translations by Don Kenny. But only the following six volumes were issued:

1. *Dodesukaden*
2. *Sanshiro Sugata* and *No Regrets for Our Youth*
3. *One Wonderful Sunday* and *Drunken Angel*

4. *The Quiet Duel* and *Stray Dog*
5. *The Idiot* and *Ikiru*
6. *The Hidden Fortress* and *The Bad Sleep Well*
The following scripts have also been published:
Richie, Donald, ed. and trans. *Ikiru.* London: Lorrimer, 1968; New York: Simon and Schuster, 1969.
————. *Rashomon.* New York: Grove Press, 1969.
————. *Seven Samurai.* London: Lorrimer 1970; New York: Simon and Schuster, 1971.